Love you, Joanne!
Belinda McDaniel

Magnificent Strength of Heart
A Memoir of War, Faith and Family

Belinda Perez McDanel

MCDANEL MEDIA
courageous stories
Bakersfield, CA

Copyright © 2020 by Belinda McDanel. All rights reserved.

Magnificent Strength of Heart: a memoir of war, faith and family
Published by McDanel Media
PO Box 5712, Bakersfield CA 93308-5712
www.belindamcdanel.com

ISBN 978-1-7359405-0-2   Paperback
ISBN 978-1-7359405-1-9   eBook
ISBN 978-1-7359405-2-6   Hardback

All rights reserved. No part of this book may be reproduced, stored in a retrieval system, or transmitted in any form or by any means—electronic, mechanical, photocopy, recording, or any other—except in brief quotations in printed reviews, without the prior permission of the publisher.

Scripture quotations taken from the New English Bible, copyright ©Cambridge University Press and Oxford University Press 1961, 1970. All rights reserved.

Some names and identifying details have been changed to protect the privacy of individuals.

Cover design by Scarlyn Feliz

Printed in the United States of America

Based on a true story.

Dedication

To my family who walked together with me during our perilous journey in El Salvador.

Noe Perez

Elida Perez

Pearl Perez Tapanes

Amanda Perez Gardner

Foreword

When we read or hear the word "missionary," do our eyes glaze over or do our minds think judgmental thoughts? Or do we think of a missionary as a servant or a saint who has been called but still do not reflect on how much that missionary is a real person? Maybe we do not comprehend what the on-the-ground, livin'-la-vida-loca, definition of "missionary" is, but Belinda Perez shares with us what we are rarely privy to: a young life as the daughter of missionaries and her own mission service of imparting the good news of Christ's love in down-to-earth stories based sometimes in harsh reality.

I first learned of the Perez family from my Aunt Elma and her Mexican Baptist Church in Anaheim, California. They were supporters of the Perez family's missionary work. Periodically, the interdenominational missionary training school, Christians in Action, sent out a newsletter which I would read with great interest and curiosity. In fact, I was inspired and felt called to attend the same missionary school in Long Beach, California, which the Perez family attended. Little did I know that my training would lead me, at age 21, to El Salvador and to the welcoming Perez family when they lived in the Isidro Menendez neighborhood in downtown San Salvador. While waiting for my missionary visa so I could travel to Cartagena, Colombia, I lived with the Perez family and worked between Guatemala and El Salvador for almost a year. I well remember that bumpy, unpredictable five-hour trip that Belinda describes.

In El Salvador I made local neighborhood visits to share the good news of Christ. I also recall being at the Perez home after a day's work, fearfully hearing bombs explode somewhere in the night. I must admit that I was truly naïve about the political situation developing in El Salvador from 1977 to 1978. But I was able to experience that country in its beauty before it was ravaged by civil war.

In the safety of our homes we have listened to news stories about this or that country, but unlike Forrest Gump, rarely do we have occasion to live in the midst of extreme historical moments, of political and social troubles. Yet such is the experience of Belinda and her family who as foreigners, yes, missionaries, were sent to share God's love with other people who lived in a country without peace, whose inhabitants may have felt, "How can I stop long enough to realize I am loved if I am in the midst of my country's dangerous civil war?"

Belinda's testimony is significant and valuable for the fearful times which we ourselves are experiencing in the midst of U.S. American political fissures as exemplified by our 2020 presidential election. We can learn from brave souls who crossed the borders of cultures, customs and politics in order to realize that life is not always like the idyllic television program of the mid-20th century, *Father Knows Best*. Following God's call and a life of service may place us in dangerous situations.

Just ask Jesus.

–Vivian Marie Varela Lugo
Missionary to Central and South America
Member of All Saints Episcopal Church in Pasadena, California
Lay leader in the Latino/a Episcopal community
November, 2020

presidential election. We can learn from brave souls who crossed the borders of cultures, customs and politics in order to realize that life is not always like the idyllic television program of the mid-20th century, *Father Knows Best*. Following God's call and a life of service may place us in dangerous situations.

Just ask Jesus.

–Vivian Marie Varela Lugo
Missionary to Central and South America
Member of All Saints Episcopal Church in Pasadena, California
Lay leader in the Latino/a Episcopal community
November, 2020

Acknowledgements

Thank you to family and friends who listened to me talk endlessly about this book when it was just a dream. Special gratitude goes to Bruce, Ben, Briana, Noe Perez, Elida Perez, Amanda Gardner. Also to Cristina, John Noe, Laura, Dani, Emily, Natalie, Judi and Vivian.

Thank you to therapists Mary Royer, Fonda Hart and Karen Kniffen.

Thank you mentors and life coaches Sheryl Fleisher, Kathy McIlhargey, Perry Rhue and Jim Smith.

For all the encouragement about writing, thank you to Jeff Goins and Tribe Writers.

Thank you to editor Darlene Stock Stotler, graphic designer Scarlyn Feliz and videographers at Captivating Videography.

And finally, thank you to Ana who protected me and my sisters.

Introduction

Woven in the wild stories of my childhood is my spiritual journey, from being a skeptic to becoming spiritually awakened. Deep inside, I found a part of me that knows information and feelings but can't explain how it knows. This is the part that gets mocked by my rational mind. This is the part that told me to write this book. This is also the part where I found an unlimited source of strength. My hope is that you connect to an unlimited source of strength, if you haven't already. Then share your amazing stories with me.

When life hits you with adversity, sometimes you react without thinking. What happens when you really think about it? What process gets you through? What do you do when you get stuck in pain? How do you cope, act and then triumph? I address these questions using stories from my childhood.

To prepare for this book, I typed up my journals from 1978 to 1979 in a database. I researched the University of Maryland's terrorist database.[1] I had many memories of horrific incidents but very few dates. I matched, as best I could, my memories with the data. The University of Maryland tracked four kinds of violent incidents: armed assaults, kidnappings, assassinations and bombings. We lived in El Salvador from January 1977 to May 1979. During our time, there were:

    61 Bombings

    18 Abductions

    21 Armed Assaults

    26 Assassinations

I gathered data from my family through interviews. One year, Dad gave me copies of all our missionary newsletters from 1975 to 1980. I found useful a 17-page paper I wrote in high school about El Salvador. In addition, I attended a class on Liberation Theology at Asbury Theological Seminary. This was the perfect research to understand the ideology of the terrorists and base camps. The most recent preparation for writing this book was a life coaching class I attended called *A Brain Approach to Learning*. This is where I found words to describe my internal dialogue among my head, heart, gut and spirit.

Disclaimer: I remember some traumatic events with vivid detail. Other stories I remember in general. I have added some detail to create a cohesive story. Books and newspapers were a great resource, especially *Encyclopedia of Kidnappings*. The only story I could not verify was the kidnapping of a nine-year-old girl. Three of my family members do not remember that story.

I hope these stories give you strength.

Contents

Chapter 1 Changing Narrative 1
Chapter 2 The Hero Narrative 13
Chapter 3 Cold War and Strong Perez Woman 25
Chapter 4 Loss in Rapid Succession 39
Chapter 5 Guatemala & Reader's Digest Stories 51
Chapter 6 Are We Rich? 61
Chapter 7 Sometimes You Fight 73
Chapter 8 Passport Stamps and Twinkies 81
Chapter 9 Hiding in the Theater 95
Chapter 10 Behind the U.S. American Embassy 107
Chapter 11 Pure in Heart 119
Chapter 12 Kidnapping 135
Chapter 13 Close Call 147
Chapter 14 Factory Bomb 157
Chapter 15 Detained in the Country 171
Chapter 16 Magnificent Heart 179
Epilogue 187

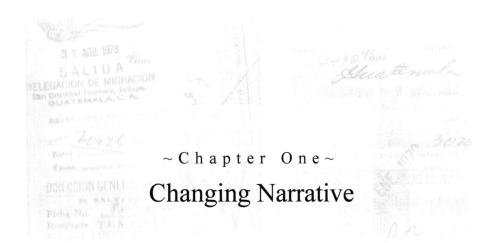

~Chapter One~
Changing Narrative

No one would believe us if we told them our stories.
Elida Perez

Never in a million years would I expect that kidnappings would have anything to do with me. How on earth did Salvadoran soldiers think we were involved?

I was 13 years old and my parents were missionaries sent to establish, or plant as some call it, a fledgling Christian congregation. But now someone was thinking the worst and he stood in an olive drab, military uniform with a scowl on his face.

"It will be an adventure," Mom sounded excited every time we moved to another country. I think she said this to convince us another move was what we wanted. But I never wanted to move.

I hated leaving friends. But this is what happens when you had adventurous and risk-taking parents who loved to travel.

We arrived in El Salvador on January 18, 1977 in a red-and-white 1972 Volkswagen van complete with red-and-white checkered curtains. It was Dad's 37th birthday. The van was bursting at the seams with all our worldly goods: large green suitcases, a black guitar case, a skateboard, boxes of books and even a bed frame perched on the roof. Before we arrived, we didn't know anything about kidnappings or a military government. We didn't know that El Salvador was in the throes of a civil war and that seven terrorist groups—one of them Catholic—were fighting in the streets. But like a shock of cold water on our faces, we would soon feel the sting.

⋆ • ⋆ • ⋆ • ⋆

Mom stands with one hand on her hip and one hand pointing to the door, "Let's go. We've got some errands to do in the city. Move it! Move it!" When Mom raises her voice, we race to the van. My two sisters, Pearl and Amanda, make us the Three Musketeers. Pearl "the older," Amanda "the younger" and that leaves me in the middle.

We drive on a paved road with houses on both sides that reveal a mid-century architecture; it looks like any other U.S. American neighborhood. Ours is the modest light green, post-WWII cinder-block house with two bedrooms. The heart of the city is about 20 miles from our suburban neighborhood, Scandia.

The carport is framed by a dark-green wrought iron gate. All the houses down the street have wrought iron bars on the windows for protection.

As we leave the neighborhood, traffic starts to slow down. I look ahead to see a military checkpoint blocking the two-lane road. When we reach a full stop, soldiers in green uniforms stand on each side of our van walking casually between cars. Rifles hang by straps on their shoulders as they strut about. A few cars ahead, a driver hands over a driver's license to a soldier who looks at the ID then waves them on. I'm curious and look out the window to see people strolling on the sidewalk. No one seems upset by the soldiers but I'm wondering, why is everyone so calm? Because I'm feeling alarm. Is it because they're so used to this kind of military presence? The line moves fast. Good, I hate waiting.

When we arrive at the front of the line, the soldier motions for us to pull over to the roadside. Soldiers surround us. They don't even ask for our passports; they just wave their arms to direct us out of the van. Some stood guard over us while others began to search the van. We line up shoulder to shoulder on the dirt: Mom, Amanda, Pearl, and me. Dad is on the other side of the van talking to the scowling lieutenant in charge.

To look at us you wouldn't know we are from the United States of America. We're of Mexican and Native American heritage. We blend in with all the other tan, dark-haired people.

The only feature that makes us noticeable is our height; Mom and Dad are tall compared to the people here. Dad is 5-feet 8-inches and Mom is 5-feet 5-inches. It's strange to watch soldiers be suspicious of Dad. If they only knew him, they wouldn't look at him like this.

֍ • ֎ • ֍ • ֎

I loved Dad. He was devoted to his family and he adored Mom. In contrast to the Latin American macho culture, Dad served Mom. Her intense dark-chocolate eyes rimmed with long lashes moved him as soon as the words were out of her mouth, "Honey, could you get me some [insert item here]?" And Dad ran out the door and within a few minutes he returned with ice cream, chocolate, root beer floats, watermelon or whatever was her fancy. Dad was a soldier-turned-missionary. He fought in the Vietnam conflict. Born in 1941 in Texas, Dad was the son of a carpenter and a full Native American Mom. I once asked Dad why he wanted to be a missionary. He looked at me with his hazel-green eyes and smiled, "I always dreamed of traveling. That's why I joined the Army. Then I felt the Lord call me to the ministry. Dad's first response to God after the call was, 'What about the girls?' He heard the Lord say, "I'll take care of the girls."

֍ • ֎ • ֍ • ֎

Soldiers surround us. They search the van. My mind goes wild: How on earth are we going to get out of this? What's going on? What's going to happen next? Then my gut starts to expect the worst: Will I walk away from this? Will someone in my family die today? I don't know why, but my next reaction is to tighten my skinny stomach, like I'm facing a bully in a school fight. I feel dread down to my core and an energy flush through my veins. I stand and wait. It's a battle between my mind and my gut. My mind wants to stay calm. My gut wants to panic. But I must wait for the moment to pass. Then I wait for the all-clear signal from Dad. Wait for the moment we can return to safety.

The lieutenant talks to Dad. I can't hear their words, but I see their mouths moving. The soldier looks disappointed, waves his hand toward the van. They let us go. Dad nods in our direction. One small wave from Dad's hand is the all-clear signal. Mom grabs Amanda by the hand. Pearl pushes me in front of her and places her hand on my back; we sprint to the van almost stepping on each other. We drive off towards the city. My heart is pounding as I look out the windows to see crowded city streets with vendors selling their wares: pineapple spears, mango slices, watermelons on tropical fruit carts, creamy pink frozen-fruit bars and vibrant orange and yellow macramé bracelets. And people are lined up to take the bus.

∽ • ∾ • ∽ • ∾

"Eat your orange" with a thump, Mom puts an orange on the dining room table in front of me. Oranges are cheap; we eat lots of them. We gather around a six-foot long folding table with gray metal folding chairs on a cold tile floor. This is our home and we will be here for 11 months.

Dad peels his orange with a knife leaving the peel in a long spiraling ring. His voice echoes in the mostly empty house, "A businessman was kidnapped recently in a red and white van, just like ours."

Everyone stops in mid, orange-eating motion and looks to Dad. Then we look to each other in disbelief with jaws dropping. Dad's face is calm, "That van even had the same curtains as ours. He was a local hero, a rags-to-riches story." I'm watching Dad fascinated by his skill and patience with the orange peel. I could never do that. He cut the orange in half then fourths until each piece was bite sized.

Pearl lowers her eyebrows, "No wonder the soldiers hassled us." She puts her hair behind her ear leaving the other side to dangle in front of her.

Dad reports what he heard, "Rich people in El Salvador are targeted by terrorists. The rich pay millions of dollars to kidnappers who are part of a terrorist group. This is how they fund their rebellion."

Mom bites her orange peel and then peels it with her long, strong nails. She opens the orange with her thumbs as orange juice squirts on her face, arms, and on the table. She wipes her hands and face with a napkin. She eats the orange in odd slices then some of the peel and says, "All the vitamins are in the peel.

You should have…" Mom trails off. As usual, she doesn't finish her sentence as she takes another bite. She wipes her hands and face with a new napkin adding to the pile of napkins in front of her. None of us girls are as meticulous as Dad. And none of us are as outrageous as Mom.

"But why would they kidnap a local hero?" I asked.

Pearl adds, "I thought this was a fight between the poor and the rich. A poor man becomes rich and then gets kidnapped because he is rich? What on earth?"

"It doesn't make sense," Pearl and I say in unison. We smile and then bump each other elbow to elbow.

"You assume terrorism makes sense. Why would you …" Mom trails off again.

I shake my head. I keep thinking I can't believe soldiers would think we might have something to do with a kidnapping. They searched *our van* like we were common criminals.

Then I become grateful Dad is a trained soldier because he knows what to do in times of war. Right away he starts training the family. In an unusually loud and bossy tone of voice, that's just as bossy as my mom's, he speaks clearly, "Next time we stop at a roadblock, look down. Don't look the soldiers in their eyes. You don't want them to think you're challenging their authority. When you hear gunfire, *HIDE*." Dad emphasized. "Drop to the floor, or get behind something—a wall, a piece of furniture—something." He clears his throat and raises his eyebrows, "Don't go to the window to see what's happening." All three of us girls laugh. Dad is never silly, and he looks silly right now with his eyes wide and incredulous looking. We stop our giggling and become serious, showing respect. I feel like laughing some more but I hold it in. Dad continues, "… that's how you get yourself killed. Don't stick your head out like a dummy. You have to think."

With a far-away look in his eyes Dad recalls, "I remember when I was in Vietnam. We would march all day. At night we would stop and find a place to rest. The first thing some men would do is to light up a cigarette. What a stupid thing to do. They just gave away our position to the enemy. Don't ever reveal your position. At night, keep the lights turned off. When the lights are on people see right into the house clear as day. If you turn on the lights, make sure to close the curtains first." Dad is always calm, yet so passionate about protecting his family. Dad ends his training with this: "Think! If you don't, it can get you killed. Don't do anything to draw attention to yourself. Don't be stupid. It can get you killed."

Don't be stupid.

෴ • ෴ • ෴ • ෴

The very next day we drive into the city with all five Perezes: Mom, Dad, Pearl, Amanda and me. Again, the soldiers stop us at the military checkpoint. The same thing is happening. The armed soldiers motion for us to pull over. We pile out of the van and stand in the same order: Mom, Amanda, Pearl, and me. Soldiers surround us and search the van. This time we follow Dad's instructions: eyes looking to the dirt on the ground.

The soldiers seem frustrated when they don't find weapons or contraband in the van. The lieutenant yells at us, "Take down those curtains." He grabs one of the curtains by the corner and unhooks it. He points to the rest of the curtains ordering us, "Take them down!"

We're still suspects in a kidnapping and that blows my mind. When they release us, we pile into the van fast. Before we drive off, I reach and unhinge the spring hooks that hold the red-and-white checkered curtains. Pearl reaches on the opposite side and unhinges them. Amanda stretches to reach the curtains in the back.

We drive a short distance, then park at the post office. Dad runs inside to check the mailbox while we wait. This was before cell phones and email. He returns carrying a stack of envelopes. Our only connection to home is letters and exorbitantly expensive phone calls.

We drive out of the post office parking lot but don't realize there is a protest. People in the streets shout and chant. Our van has no place to go but straight toward the crowd. Dad tries to get the van through the crowd.

Trembling, Mom says, "Noe. Get us out of here." Dad's name means Noah in Spanish. It's pronounced "No-ee," not "No."

Dad revs the van and honks the horn trying to inch forward. He answers Mom with his jaw clinched, "Elida, I'm trying." People walk in the middle of the street and soon surround the van. Just at the other side of the window are vehement faces—mostly men in slacks and button-up shirts. The crowd pushes the van with their hands. Dad edges us forward. The crowd starts rocking the van and shouting. Dad honks the horn as he pushes the van through the crowd. We break free. The whole ordeal lasts only a few minutes, but time moves in slow motion when my heart is beating fast. I take deep breaths. I need to calm my heart. Talk about a close call.

It's hard to follow Dad's instructions sometimes because I hold the shock of it all inside. I feel a small lump in my throat, yet I remind myself that we're all okay. Still, I feel a small warm tear running down the side of my face. I wipe it away quickly before anyone notices.

Welcome to El Salvador.

꧁ • ꧂ • ꧁ • ꧂

Missionaries love to tell stories to each other, the sending agency and the supporters back home. The challenge in El Salvador was to tell enough of the story to garner serious prayer support but not so much that we'd get into trouble with the government.

In the first missionary newsletter to all the supporters Dad wrote, "Pray for God's protection over us. We have had three close calls with protests and a shootout; also, our house has been broken into twice in three weeks."

The local Christians warned us not to say too much about the political situation here. Dad didn't write about the kidnapping or our run-ins with soldiers because if you express any opinion about politics or criticize the government, they assume you're a communist. They'll search for your connections to Russia. This was the 1970s—the era of the Cold War where Russia was recruiting as many countries as it could for communism. The United States was recruiting as many countries as it could for democracy. Both were collecting allies. If you were suspected of being a communist in El Salvador, you would get black-listed, which means they would kill you.

⋅•⋅•⋅•⋅

For a long time, I never used the word trauma to describe my life. For me, life was a collection of stories. I started using the word trauma in my 40s after talking to Christian therapists. Thank God for Christian counselors because talking to them was healing to my heart, mind and body. The important part is not the details of my narrative, but the process I went through to develop it.

In this book, I will take you further through my changing narrative, not so much from the perspective of a therapist but from the perspective of one who has learned resilience in the school of hard knocks. My hope is that you find strength, inner strength, spiritual strength, not by using my narrative but by discovering your own. But first, we must start with my early childhood where my narrative begins.

~Chapter Two~
The Hero Narrative

Resilience is transmissible
by sharing the stories that inspire us we can pass it on.
Giles Duley[2]

An internal locus of control is when a person feels powerful in their world and can be proactive. An external locus of control is when a person feels powerless and tends to be reactive.

As we were growing up, Pearl and I were constantly competing, wrestling on the floor, racing in the pool or running through the grass. Pearl won most of the time because she was bigger and stronger than my skinny frame. Still, I made her earn it. We felt powerful in this world. After Amanda was born, by the time she was five years old, she joined in our love for adventure and solving mysteries. We played make believe as cowboys, or even better, we played spies. Everything was a weapon. A stick or a broom magically transformed into a rifle or a sword. We pretended to have government secrets and we were the heroines, running barefoot through our childhood. The world was our domain. We were its master.

I look back at my childhood and I think about the stories I tell myself, the running narrative in my head. Life was full of experiences both good and bad. What about your childhood? What did you tell yourself so you could make sense of everything? Especially the things in life that were unexpected and cruel. Pearl, Amanda and I were learning to be capable. As our imaginative playtimes gave way to homework and self awareness, we took responsibility and solved the problems in our world. We were heroes.

❧ • ☙ • ❧ • ☙

The windows of the car are open. It's a sunny day in 1967. Mom, Pearl and I are riding in Mom and Dad's red 1966 Impala on a road trip from Texas to Nebraska. We're visiting Uncle Lee and Aunt Monica who's about to deliver her third baby.

"We're gonna get in trouble." I whisper in my big sister's ear. We're both sitting in the back seat with no seatbelts.

"No, we're not," Pearl whispers back.

I open my mouth, "But …"

She puts her finger over my lips and insists, "No, it will be fun. Come on, let me shampoo your hair. Just pretend with me." She opens the peanut butter jar with some effort. Her six-year-old hands are barely able to grip the lid while her face is straining as she lets out a little grunt, "Ugh."

"But we're gonna get in trouble." I look to the front seat where Mom is driving our new red Impala.

"Oh, don't be such a party pooper." Pearl nudges me with her elbow.

Pearl is 20 months older than me. I adore my big sister and I love to have fun with her. I just hate when we get in trouble and get our butts slapped.

"Come on, hold still," as she scoops a big lump of peanut butter on my short black straight hair and massages my head. I stop thinking about getting in trouble. This is fun.

I thrust my hand into the peanut butter jar and scoop up some peanut butter. I pretend that I must take a bath, so I rub it on my arms and legs. Pearl giggles and starts putting peanut butter on her arms and legs, too.

"It's my turn to wash your hair," I whisper.

Belinda (left) with Pearl

"Okay but hurry up." She sits still for only a minute and starts reaching toward the seat in front of her making her back arch. I see her idea. This is perfect for finger painting on the seat in front of us like a huge blank paper. I grab a blob and lump it on top of her short black hair.

Rub, rub, rub. I need to wash her hair good. "Okay, it's done. Go play now."

Pearl jumps to the floor of the car and crouches on her legs. "Look, I'm drawing our house," Pearl points.

I lick my hands and create a paste. Then I join her on the floor of the car sitting cross-legged. "Oh, look, a tree, see?" as I create a masterpiece.

She paints a house. I paint a flower. We look at each other lean in, our foreheads touch, and we giggle.

Suddenly Mom's head is turning towards us and I get this sinking feeling in my stomach. Pearl and I freeze. Mom glances over her shoulder and then stomps on the brakes. Pearl and I fly forward into the vinyl seat. We bounce back. When the car is at a full stop, she yells at us. "What! What have you done? You little rascals!" With clinched teeth she spits out, "I can't believe it!" And she turns the steering wheel.

Pearl and I look at each other, eyes wide. "See, I told you we're going to get in trouble." I say as I lick my fingers.

Mom pulls into a gas station and the car jerks as she drives over the driveway. She's mad. A man comes to her window.

"How may I help you, ma'am?" He looks at us in the backseat, bursts out laughing and slaps his knee with his hand. "I'll clean up the car and you clean up the girls. You can park around the back close to the bathrooms."

"Thank you so much," Mom didn't sound mad. But she parked the car with a jerk. "Come on you little troublemakers." Mom opened our door.

I think, for sure, we're going to get a spanking. In a little bathroom with a little sink Mom cleans us both. She didn't spank us or yell. Whew!

Some say either you have an internal locus of control or external. I say there are times in our lives when we feel more powerful and other times we don't. I felt powerful as a child especially when an adult asked me to help them. There, in the gas station bathroom I felt a little guilty pleasure because we got away with it.

≼ • ≽ • ≼ • ≽

1968, Corpus Christi, Texas

Grandpa Damian Peña leans forward from the worn couch and says in the raspy old voice, "Boy, go get me some rain." His grandmother was Lipan Apache and Grandpa looks Native American with long dark hair and tan skin.

"Grannnnnnpa! I'm not a boy."

With a snap of his fingers and a wave of his arm, "You have short hair like a boy."

"Grannnnnnpa! I'm not a boy." I stomp my right foot.

Grandpa Damian Pena

Grandpa smiles revealing his missing tooth. "Okay, okay. You're not a boy. Now go get me some rain." I know what he means. Grandpa is asking for a glass of water.

From behind me I could hear Grandpa Peña still teasing me, "You have short hair like a boy."

Heading toward the kitchen I shout back. "But I'm not a boy!"

As I take each step toward Grandpa across the worn wooden floor, I say to myself, "Careful, don't spill the water. Careful, don't spill the water." I'm looking at my bare feet as I take each step. "Here you go, Grandpa."

"Pearl and me want to go outside to play. Can we go outside? Pleeeeeease?"

"Hold on a minute," Grandpa takes a big gulp of water, "AAAHHHH." He smiles revealing his high cheekbones and a sparkle in his chocolate brown eyes. "That's some good rain, Mija. Yeah, you girls go play outside."

Mija is a Spanish term of endearment. It means my daughter and it pronounced *me-ha*.

"Let's go." Pearl and I turn on our heels and run out the door leaving the old screen door slamming behind me and Grandpa's shouts, "Don't play on my truck."

We jump off the porch onto the soft grass on our bare feet. Grandma and Grandpa's house is so much fun! They have a garage with tools leaning along the wall, shovels, rakes and on the counter, I see rusty pliers and shiny hammers. The big backyard even has a pigeon coop. When we get bored, we play with the birds. There is even a crawl space under the white wooden house. They don't have sidewalks and there is a ditch running across the front of the lawn.

"I have an idea," Pearl smiles, "Let's play Tarzan and Jane. I'll be Tarzan. You be Jane." She dances on the lawn.

"Okay, that sounds like fun." I make a twirl and a cartwheel. The grass feels soft on my bare feet.

Trees always look like they are ready to hug and Grandpa had this massive tree with white bark peeling off the side and its skinny branches resembling slumped shoulders.

"This tree is perfect. We can swing from the branches," Pearl said.

Pearl gets on her tiptoes and stretches her body as tall as it can go to reach the lowest branch.

"Belinda, come here. Climb on my shoulders. Come on."

Pearl crouches down like we're playing leapfrog and I climb on her shoulders and straddle her neck. She steadies herself and lifts me with my feet dangling in front of her chest. I reach up as tall as I can, and I still can't reach the branches. Even with Pearl on her tiptoes, we still can't reach the branches. She let me down off her shoulders. We both sit on the ground with gravel prickling our legs right below our shorts as our backs lean against the large tree trunk.

Pearl puts her head down and I put my head in my hands, thinking. How can we do this?

Pearl lifts her head, "Let's climb on Grandpa's truck."

"Noooooo. We're gonna get in trouble. Grandpa said not to play on his truck." I look to the house feeling certain Grandpa heard us.

"Aw, come on. It's the only way to reach the branches."

She's right. If we're going to play Tarzan and Jane, we must reach the branches.

"Okaaaaay."

Pearl jumps to her feet and rushes to the back of the old black Chevy truck and climbs on the bumper. I struggle to lift the weight of my five-year-old body. After we both climb up, we stand on the bumper and dive into the back of the truck and fall on our heads and then fall sideways. We laugh.

Pearl runs to the truck cab, climbs on up on top and stands on the roof. I follow her. She reaches a branch from the tree and grabs one.

"See, I knew this would work. Are you ready? You need to hang on to my waist real tight," with a determined look on her face.

"Okay, hold still."

"Tighter."

With the full weight of our little five- and six-year-old bodies on one branch, we take an unexpected dive. Not very much like a swinging Tarzan and Jane.

Pearl lands on top of me and rolls over on her side laughing.

I start crying.

"Why are you crying?"

"You landed on top of me."

Pearl lifts her hand to cover her mouth, rolls over laughing again.

"Owwww."

That night, we change into our pajamas. I see that I have a huge bruise that takes up my entire side. If Mom sees this, she's going to ask me about it. If she finds out that we were playing on Grandpa's truck, we'll get in trouble. I turn my body sideways to hide my bruise. I don't want to get in trouble.

This is family covering for each other so that we don't get yelled at. Sometimes mothers don't understand the important work of children. We explore. Everything. In case someone needs to know, we have gathered the information. Who do adults call on when they need someone to crawl into a small space? The children, of course. For instance, if someone locks themselves out of their house, the children know just which window can be jimmied. They say, "They're only children." But we know things. Sometimes adults don't understand our powers, especially girl power.

+☙ • ❧ • ☙ • ❧

About 50 years ago, people called girls Tomboys if they were athletic and adventurous. If you were the kind of girl who liked to sit quietly indoors and play with a pile of dolls, you were just a girl. I never understood girls who weren't interested in jumping, running or exploring the roof. Pearl and I loved all that. We're curious and that used to get us in all kinds of trouble.

We lived in a world that was ours to explore. Together we have explored the moon and used branches as swings in the jungle or weapons. In our world there were no limits because we soared in our imagination. I loved having Pearl as a big sister because she'd beat up bullies at school who picked on me. Sometimes she picked on me, but to be fair, when she did, I got back at her. Pearl and I really got into it. We wrestled on the floor for fun but sometimes it turned ugly. We always made up afterward. We had to. Who was going to protect me from the bullies but Pearl? This is family being your protector one moment and being mean to you the next.

One day we were playing in the living room and Pearl punched me in the gut. I punched her back. She pulled my hair; I pulled her hair. We didn't say anything it was just a lot of grunts and huffs. And before we knew it, we were rolling on the living room floor punching each other. I don't remember why we were fighting. I knew enough as a child if somebody hit you, you must hit back.

Mom walked into the living room to see Pearl and I rolling around on the floor. She screamed at us and it caught us by surprise, "Stop that right now!" Mom grabbed my arm and yanked me away from Pearl. At the same time, she grabbed Pearl's arm and made her get back on her feet.

"I don't want to see you hitting each other. EVER AGAIN. Do you hear me?" She raised her voice then released our arms. Ouch that hurt. I rub my arm.

With one hand on her hip and one hand pointing, Mom stood there. "In this world you will have enough to fight about. Out there." She points to the front door. She put her finger in our faces again, "But family sticks together. We don't fight each other. You'll have enough to fight in the world. We're family and we count on each other to be there. Don't fight." She paused and then with the last exclamation, "I don't E-V-E-R want to see you do that again."

Pearl and I stood up straight as if we were at attention. Our hands latched behind our backs and our heads bowed slightly showing Mom respect.

In unison we reply, "Yes, ma'am."

"Now go play. And I better not see you hitting your sister. Or I'll give you something to cry about." She swings her hand in a motion like when we get a spanking.

That was a huge moment for me because Mom defined family. Mom was teaching me about enemies in the world. Family is not an enemy. We will have enough enemies outside our house. But here, we don't fight each other. I never hit Pearl after that. She hit me a few more times when Mom wasn't looking. I rolled up in a ball on the floor not because I was powerless, but because I refused to use my power to hit her. She wailed on me and I just took it but soon it stopped. I guess it wasn't the same when I didn't hit back. You fight the enemy out in the world, but the enemy is not in your house. I chose not to hit back. I could have hit her but I decided in my heart never do that again. That was a life lesson for me. This is learning what it means to be family. I learned one overarching rule: We have to stick together as a family because the enemy was somewhere outside the front door.

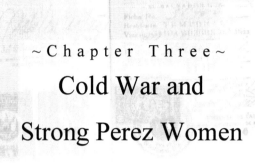

~ Chapter Three ~

Cold War and Strong Perez Women

Perez women are strong. And don't you forget it.
Elida Perez

Moms are supposed to be nurturing and soft, but sometimes you need a mom who is strong and determined.

Mom was feisty and I loved her. She was harder to love than Dad because she was so bossy and I didn't like it. I loved to watch her defend me in her anger, but, boy, I hated when her anger was turned on me. Born in 1944 in Corpus Christi, Texas, her family came from long-time residents of Texas. According to Grandma Matilda Peña, our family had been in Texas since before it was a state. Grandma used to say, "There were no white people back then. It was just us and the Indians."

Combine Mom's feistiness with her great storytelling and she was entertaining. She enjoyed a small audience. I think one reason I remember so many stories is because Mom told these very same stories. One of my favorite ones is about Mom in El Salvador when she went to the market, the mercado, which is more like a farmer's market than a grocery store. The mercado was huge with every color of fruit and vegetable that you could imagine, and some you'd probably never seen before: oranges, mangos, avocados, pineapples, watermelons and papayas. I never liked going because it smelled of rotting fruit.

On one of our trips to the mercado, Mom was double-parked on the street behind a long line of double-parked cars. She took Ana, who worked for my parents. Ana jumped out of the car to buy a few things at the mercado while Mom waited in the van. A police officer approached Mom. He said he was going to give her a ticket.

She pointed her finger right up in his face, "Oh, no, you're not!"

He raised his eyebrows and his eyes got big with surprise.

Mom set him straight, "If you're going to give me a ticket, you have to give tickets to every single car that is double-parked!"

The police officer wouldn't give her a ticket if she bribed him. But Mom refused to give him a bribe. She had made her point.

In my mind, I could see Mom pointing her finger at all the cars in front of her. I imagine Mom with a determined look on her face that says, *I dare you to mess with me.* Mom didn't get a ticket.

Mom was amazing in a crisis. You could see the fighter rise up in her. She took on any challenge that life gives. Nothing is too big. In fact, the bigger the crisis, the more she shined and that made me feel secure. Screaming and barking orders was comforting to me because she got everyone moving in the same direction. If I ever saw Mom quiet during a crisis, her quietness scared me.

Sometimes I would wish for a mom who was more nurturing and sensitive, who likes to talk about feelings and fluffy stuff. But I don't know what I would have done if I had a mom who cried in front of soldiers. I look back and I'm grateful. Mom always took charge in terrible situations and told us how we were going to get through them.

※ • ※ • ※ • ※

On February 6, 1977, terrorists assassinated Salvadoran colonel Jose Rene Chacon. This wasn't even three weeks after the military checkpoint incident in our red Volkswagen (VW) van. The Colonel represented the military government backed by the United States. The terrorists who killed him represented the rebels backed by Russia. Without knowing it, we had stepped into the Cold War.

I had never heard of the military running a government, but later I learned that the politicians here are ex-military. They use soldiers to control the people. This explains why we would see so many military trucks full of soldiers on their way to different parts of the city. I'm used to a military that protects the people. In El Salvador, I'm afraid of soldiers because when tensions are high, they point their machine guns at us from the back of a truck. When I say us, I mean everybody on the street who is not in a military uniform.

We got used to stopping at the military checkpoints and seeing soldiers on our drive into the city. We got used to the long line of cars taking up city blocks. We got used to seeing men in military uniforms on city streets and major intersections. As the kidnapping of the businessman in the red VW van faded from people's memories, soldiers didn't always hassle us. The news media had shifted attention from the recent kidnapping of the businessman to protests, riots and the assassination of the Colonel.

In response to kidnappings by terrorists, the Salvadoran government formed a death squad. I learned a term called *los desaparecidos,* disappeared ones. When people suddenly go missing, you know they were killed. All kinds of people disappeared: businessmen, terrorists and people who were critical of the government. We can't say anything about the government because we don't want to become one of *los desaparecidos*.

In 1977, the Salvadoran government used other methods as well in their fight to keep its power. They struck down protests or uprisings by shooting at protesters. My parents were downtown when a shootout broke out. They ran for cover and found shelter in a pharmacy. Right as the metal gate was lowering, they slipped in. They joined a diverse group of people inside, and waited together until the shooting stopped. The government even fought the Catholic Church since Archbishop Oscar Arnulfo Romero openly criticized the government and fought for free speech. This civil war had gone on for years, so the local people told us.

Evidence of kidnappings and assassinations decorated the city streets. The common practice was to shoot all the witnesses. So, we would drive past a location of a recent kidnapping or assassination to see a shot-up, abandoned car on the street. The surrounding buildings were decorated with evidence of heavy gunfire. I couldn't tell who had done it, the government or the terrorists. They both looked the same to me. Assassins were sent by the government to eliminate terrorists. Terrorists were sent by rebels to kidnap victims.

Doesn't history teach us this same story? When the status quo is challenged, they fight to maintain their power. Their narrative is one of survival. But for the ones disturbing the status quo, they have a vision of what the future could be. The disrupters act from a bigger picture, one where they change history.

During the first few months in El Salvador, three things happened. First, soldiers thought we were involved in a kidnapping because we owned a red-and-white VW van, the same kind of van used to kidnap a local businessman. Second, we heard on the radio about Archbishop Romero. The more we learned about Romero, the more the war began to make sense. Third, we learned about Martial Law.

Archbishop Romero used talk radio to inform the public with lists of those who were tortured or disappeared. He advocated for civil rights.[3] His disruption made him a target. The radio antenna for his show was knocked down mysteriously during our first few months in the country. That kept him off the air for a few weeks, but soon he was on the radio denouncing the actions of the government.

Key players in this terrible political story in El Salvador were the rich and the poor. The rich included 14 families who owned 95% of the wealth. I don't know if they controlled the government exactly, but they had a lot of sway. The poor organized themselves into groups. The Catholic Church took the side of the poor. When I was in El Salvador I was aware of three major terrorist groups. But I was a kid, so in my mind they were one group, the rebels. There were seven terrorist groups in El Salvador in the 1970s:

ERP	People Revolutionary Army
FPL	People's Liberation Forces (communist)
UGB	Union Guerrera Blanca
FAPU	United Popular Action Front
MER	Revolutionary Student Movement
BPR	Revolutionary Popular Bloc
FARN	Armed Forces of National Resistance

The surprise for me was that one of the terrorist groups, BPR, was Catholic. Over 60,000 people were part of this group led by Catholic priests using both nonviolent and violent means. Even now it's hard for me to call them a terrorist group, but the Salvadoran government looked at them that way. They had military-like training camps in the countryside called base camps. This was all so weird. Dad said that most people just want to go to work and live their lives. Tragically, many who were caught in the middle got killed.

The United States government wants to keep the Salvadoran military government in power, so they supply them with arms. Who is the good guy here? The helicopters I see flying overhead are probably supplied by the United States of America. The rifles that they point at us are probably U.S. American made.

The Soviet Union on the other hand wants to establish a communist government in El Salvador. They will use force if they must. Most of the seven terrorist organizations are communist or socialist. I can't help but wonder if they get their weapons from Russia. One thing is for certain: a civil war is happening in El Salvador.

∽ • ∾ • ∽ • ∾

This is where life gets interesting. Picture a civil war, a feisty mom, a soldier-turned-missionary dad, and me in a medical emergency. It's early 1977 and I'm sick with asthma. Mom feeds me soup, but I don't want to eat. I just want to breathe. My heart is beating fast and I feel my throat closing.

I can't speak. I only say a few words at a time amongst a lot of wheezing. "Bathroom," I say.

"Noe, please carry Belinda to the bathroom. She has no strength to walk."

Dad places me gently back on the bed afterward.

I hate asthma medicine because it tastes like licorice. I hate asthma pills because of the side effects. I hate it when my heart races and my hands shake. The inhaler is good for the short term but if the asthma keeps bothering me, I need to talk to Mom. At times, I cut the pills in half or fourths, so the side effects aren't so bad. And I try not to bother Mom with this, but when my wheezing continues even after I use the inhaler, I know I'm in trouble.

If I take a deep breath, I cough. If I take a shallow breath, I don't cough but I feel like I'm not getting enough air, so I shoot for balance. I try to take a breath just deep enough to fill my lungs to mid-section, but not enough to make me cough. In bed I lie looking at the ceiling focusing on each breath.

This takes concentration.

Mom and Dad wrestle with present circumstances.

"Elida, it's late. Are you sure we can't wait until tomorrow?"

"I know the hospital is a 20-minute drive from here," Mom taps her lips with her pointer finger. "But the medicine is not helping. Belinda's wheezing so loud I can hear it from here."

"The government issued a curfew with Martial law. Anyone caught after dark is in danger," Dad says. "They shoot first and ask questions later." And their voices fade.

Dad enters my room and lifts me off the bed. I'm weak and I don't have the strength to hold up my head. He places my frail frame in the van like a rag doll. Mom, Dad, and I are on our way to the hospital at night after curfew. Is this a medical emergency? How do you handle a medical emergency and martial law during the Cold War era, all at the same time? Soldiers won't give us a chance to explain. Darkness hovers over the city, not just because the sun set but because of the heaviness of fear.

The 20-minute drive to the hospital is quiet. The whole time my heart is beating fast from medicine and fear. Tonight, I could die from asthma or I could die from a bullet. Time moves slowly as I lie on the seat of the van trying to hide. I wish I could sink into the seat and be invisible. I just want to hide where no one will see me and no one wants to kill me.

The few days in the hospital are all a blur. I wake up in a hospital bed wearing a thin cotton nightgown with a slit up the back that makes me feel naked. A nurse comes to give me a shot and I'm so glad. I don't know what's in the shot, but I can breathe again.

I see Mom sitting next to my bed. She starts giving me The Talk. I always welcome The Talk from Mom. She looks into my eyes and says:

"Belinda, listen to me. You're strong. You're a Perez woman and all Perez women are strong. We've been this way for generations. It's in your blood. Nothing can beat you. You'll get through this. You'll live to see greater days. Harder days than this. You're a Perez woman which means you're strong too. You're going to be alright. Plus, you have no choice because I am telling you to. And I am your mother!"

I close my eyes and let the strength of her words wash over me. She has such a strong character that if Mom says I can make it, there is no doubt. I absorb her words deep inside me. Mom isn't one to be tender. Perhaps that was what made The Talk so powerful. Her words pulled strength up out of me from someplace deep that I didn't know existed.

∽ • ∾ • ∽ • ∾

My family hierarchy is not what you think. Most people expect Dad to be at the top, then below him Mom, and at the bottom, the kids. Someone must be in control, right? There must be a hierarchy but that is not so in the Perez family. The hierarchy we practice is one of service. Dad serves Mom. Mom serves the kids. But the roles change depending on the situation.

Mom tends to my needs when I'm in the hospital. Dad is present to serve Mom making sure she gets bathroom breaks or gets something to eat. Pearl serves Dad by keeping an eye on Amanda or by running to get him a Pepsi. Amanda would do small errands as requested, like getting a newspaper to pass around or finding the vending machines. We stand together in a crisis and support one another. If I'm the one in crisis, I focus on getting better. Mom doesn't serve everyone. She is free to focus on me and my needs. Dad doesn't worry about me. He is concerned with Mom. Pearl and Amanda are expected to do their part as needed. The important thing is that we're together. There's no single person trying to do it all. And I'm not alone in my crisis. Adversity in life is infinitely harder when you face it alone but because of family, I was never alone. We continue this practice to this day. We serve one another's needs.

Mom says, "I have a surprise for you."

I sit up a little. My head doesn't feel as floppy on my shoulders as earlier. I feel my strength returning to me. She reaches into her purse and pulls out a hamburger.

"My favorite!"

Mom hands me the burger, "You are too skinny. Eat!"

I smile, "Thanks, Mom."

I sit up all the way to munch on my burger. We're surrounded by a curtain in a very small space. Mom is sitting on a chair next to my bed. She takes out her worn black Bible and starts reading from the marked-up pages. When I'm finished with my burger, I lay my head on the pillow and listen. Normally life is busy, but when I'm sick all the distractions of a hectic life stop, and I have time to think.

"Let me read to you from the Psalms," Mom says.

Everyone in my family reads the Bible every day. They talk about God speaking to them through the Bible and I'm a little skeptical. How can I know it's God and not just my own thoughts? I struggle with the idea that God speaks to me. Why me? Does God want to talk to me? Of all the people in the world, I have the audacity to think God wants to talk to me. Really? I don't doubt that God speaks to people because in the Bible stories God interacts with people both young and old, both male and female. But am I among them? The church teaches yes, everyone can hear. Is it true? Do I belong in the group that hears from God?

Mom's voice repeats the phrase, "His love endures forever. His love endures forever." I feel comfort as she reads, and I wonder if this is a message from God or if I'm reading into it. Does God love me here and now? I don't know, but I close my eyes and listen.

I look back now on this political climate and how Mom and Dad raised us, and I think this must have been a miracle. Mom and Dad were teaching me and my sisters about being a servant, while the climate around us was full of people helping themselves. Rich people controlling the government for purely selfish interests. Rebels kidnapping the rich to fund a rebellion.

And the assassinations of opponents. It's a big power struggle but all for selfish reasons as far as I can see.

On top of that, Mom and Dad were showing me that you could hear God's voice even when everyone else was listening to fear. I think that's what made the church attractive. Lots of people came to find comfort and peace at church. In this sense, my parents are superheroes. It's not that my parents were perfect. I have my stories of hurt feelings and having to forgive them. And they have their stories of my misbehavior and having to forgive me. But I don't focus on those stories. I know they hate when I talk like this about them as heroes, but I can't help it. I saw what I saw.

~Chapter Four~
Loss in Rapid Succession

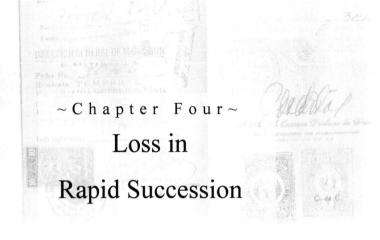

Write hard and clear about what hurts.
Ernest Hemingway[4]

Loss in rapid succession leaves you breathless and stunned on the ground. The question is: do I have the strength to get up, yet again, knowing something else might knock me down?

How did I get to El Salvador in 1977? It's the Cold War and I'm sick as a dog. I stayed in the hospital for days, at times alone with my thoughts. The last thing I remember was traveling a lot with my parents in the United States in 1975 after they completed missionary training school. We traveled for one year in a green VW bug. Every week we were in a new city so that Mom and Dad could give presentations in different churches on Sundays and Wednesdays. Sometimes Pearl and I sang together while she played the guitar. We stayed in a different home every night.

Belinda, Amanda, and Pearl in front of green VW bug

Mom trained us to be invisible in order to honor our hosts. We couldn't leave our things out. There had to be no evidence in the bathroom or living room that we were there. Our room had to be tidy and all our things kept nicely in our suitcases. Long Beach, California was our home base. Life with my parents was fun and unpredictable. A life of travel seemed normal. But then came Guatemala in 1975 and 1976, then El Salvador from 1977 to 1979. Before moving to Central America, we moved from Texas to Georgia and back again. We moved to California, then to Arizona and back again. Like Mom said, it was an adventure. But moving to another country was shocking. Having to adjust to a different culture and a different language was difficult. Travel was adventurous, but it also was a series of devastating losses.

Guatemala 1975–1976

I remember now, the devastation started in the fall of 1975. Pearl and Dad moved to Guatemala while Mom, Amanda and I stayed in Long Beach, California. (I hate this part of the story because I love the church and I don't want the church to look bad.) But the church leaders decided to separate us because Mom needed to lose weight. (Apparently, certain decision makers felt that being overweight was a sign of spiritual weakness.) My family was being torn apart. Even now, thinking about this is painful. I liked our family just the way we were, thank you. Why were they tearing us apart?

The most painful hug is the one that has goodbye attached to it. We stood on the sidewalk in front of the missionary campus in Long Beach, California, Pearl and Dad with packed suitcases. I didn't know when I would see them again. I didn't want to, but I forced my body to turn and walk away. The turning-around-and-walking-away moment was the most painful. My heart was heavy. Soon it was 1976 and the devastation continued.

🙠 • 🙢 • 🙠 • 🙢

My mom had become familiar with God speaking to her, not with an audible voice, but with an inkling in her heart. In the brisk early hours of February 4, we were still in the states. My mother was suddenly awakened.

God said to her, "I am in control." Mom glanced at her alarm clock, 3:00 a.m.

Somewhat sleepy, she answered him in her heart, "Yes, Lord, I know you are in control." She laid back on her pillow to go back to sleep.

A few minutes later God said, "I am in control."

She responded again, "Yes, Lord. You are God. You *are* in control."

Once more God said, "I am in control." She was curious about this whole exchange, but soon fell back asleep.

Later that morning I was getting ready for school when I heard a big ruckus. Thump, thump, thump. Someone was running down the hall toward our room. I heard an alarmed voice exclaim, "Elida, Elida, come quick … you have to see the news!"

Mom and I exchanged glances. I saw the concern on her face. We all ran into the common area to see the TV headline:

"Breaking News: Earthquake hits Guatemala City"

We stood stunned as the news unfolded. A 7.5 earthquake struck Guatemala City at 3:01 a.m. and thousands were feared dead. After a short report the news started repeating itself.

Our friends immediately reassured Mom. "I'm sure Noe and Pearl are fine. I wouldn't worry. Everything is going to be fine. We know God is in control." I thought to myself, it sounds like empty echoes to me. They're just trying to be supportive, but we don't know.

Mom recounted her story. Awakened three times by God telling her that *He* was in control. All of a sudden, the early morning events made sense to Mom. *Who would imagine a personal, special message from God just for you?* Mom looked at Amanda and me and said, "You need to finish getting ready for school."

The next three days were like walking in a daze, going through the motions of school and not being present. Emotions were bursting inside me, but I was quiet except with Liz, my best friend in seventh grade. She had short dark brown hair and big brown eyes. We were inseparable. I told Liz about Pearl and Dad. Her big compassionate eyes teared up. She felt my anxiety and pain. She knew I felt devastated, not that there was an earthquake, but that we didn't know if Dad and Pearl were dead or alive.

In Social Studies, the teacher got my attention. She asked the class if they heard the news about the earthquake in Guatemala. I wondered to myself, should I say anything? Do I dare reveal something precious and personal to me? Will they understand? Will anyone really care? Or is this just about world events? It's hard to know if people really care or if they are just making conversation.

I had just a second to decide whether or not to talk about Pearl and Dad. I heard myself speak up, "My father and sister are in Guatemala."

The teacher was stunned. I could see it in her eyes. She heard my words, but not my terror or my pain. She said rather coldly, "I'm sure they are okay," and redirected the class to our assignment. I shouldn't have said anything, I said to myself. See, she doesn't care. Or maybe she is stunned and doesn't know what to say to a person like me.

What happens when you feel things deeply and others don't? When your story is unbelievable, people think you just want attention or you're playing the victim. But you're not. This is really your life with all its glory and terror.

Liz saved my life. I was vulnerable with her and she saw what I saw. She didn't avoid my pain. So much pain makes people go away. People don't like their own pain, much less the pain of others. I wasn't alone because Liz stood beside me.

After three days, a ham radio operator from back east called us with a short message: "Everyone at the missionary compound in Guatemala is okay."

Mom shared the story of God talking to her again. I felt comforted by it. It was miraculous. It couldn't have been a coincidence, could it?

I felt amazed, comforted, in awe and glad to hear from God. I felt humbled that he would care for us. Yet confused—how can God be in control of such a terrible situation? Why did he let it happen at all? If he was in control, why didn't he prevent it? What does it mean that God is in control? Does it mean he will protect my family? Or does it mean he will protect the missionaries? Or will he protect only the church people? But what about the other people? What about the children? Does God care about children? Does God care about me?

Just five weeks after the earthquake, Mom, Amanda and I arrived in Guatemala.

※ • ❧ • ※ • ❧

It has felt like forever since I saw Pearl. After an eight-hour flight we're glad to stand up. There's a long line of people in front of me getting off the plane. I hold my bag and my skateboard is propped on end resting on top of my white tennis shoes with rubber tips. I stretch my neck to see beyond the long line of people in front of me. I have missed her so much.

I take a deep breath and let out a long exhale expressing my impatience. I'm looking for Dad and Pearl. Mom is holding Amanda's hand. The line moves slowly. I'm excited. I wish I could run past everybody to the front. Don't they know how important this is? But I have to wait. And I hate waiting.

Before I know it, Pearl and I hug extra tight and extra long, looking each other in the eyes. "I can't wait to talk, I have so much to tell you," Pearl smiles. Dad and I hug. His muscular body feels strong and warm. We were separated for months but it felt like years. The earth is back on its axis and all is well. I feel relieved. We're together again as a family.

We pile into the white extra-long missionary van and drive through the streets of Guatemala City. On the way home from the airport I see poor people begging on the streets and skinny stray dogs. Handicapped people sitting on filthy sidewalks, begging. People with no shoes. I'm shocked.

Pearl says, "I can't wait for you guys to see the school. You're going to love it. It's called the CAG, at least everybody calls it the CAG. The name of the school is Christian Academy of Guatemala. We have kindergarteners through 12th grade. Just wait, you'll make lots of friends."

The missionaries live on the edge of the city on a seven-acre property. It has one large mansion, two medium-size houses and some outbuildings. The large mansion is where the dorms for the men and women are located. Pearl used to stay there. After we reunited as a family, they gave us a house with three rooms, one bathroom and a small living room. The house had no decorations on the walls. Walking on the tile floors made my footsteps echo. One bedroom has two cots for Amanda and me, and there was another bedroom for Pearl with one cot. My mom and dad had their own room across from the bathroom.

I put my suitcase on the floor at the end of my cot. How do I claim this space as my own? Pearl is in the next room. I don't like that.

"Can I come in?" I stand at the entrance to her room.

"Of course."

I sit on Pearl's bed, "I missed you."

"I missed you too."

"I have so much to tell you. I don't like that we have separate bedrooms."

"Yeah me either. Let's ask Mom and Dad if we can move you into my room."

"Okay, that sounds good to me."

"You start."

"No, you start."

"Tell me about the earthquake."

Pearl lies on her back, looks straight up to the ceiling and gets a faraway look in her eyes. Then she starts to tell me. She was sleeping on the bottom bunk when the window started rattling. The whole room started shaking and she realized it was an earthquake. (You can see Pearl telling the earthquake story in her own words on YouTube[5].)

I gasp and cover my mouth with my hand.

She smiles and continues. The glass from the window was rattling. She thought for sure it was going to break. She pulled the covers up to cover herself to protect her from the glass. But she wanted to see the glass break, so she pulled the covers up right under her eyes and just watched.

"Loca." I call her *crazy* in Spanish. I don't know many Spanish words, but I know a crazy person when I see one. "Only you would find an earthquake fun."

"It lasted a long time and it was scary."

"What did you do?"

"After the shaking stopped, I went outside with everybody else. I forgot to get my shoes and it was cold, so I returned to my room to get shoes and a blanket."

"We were all scared to go indoors. First, we checked on everybody to see if everyone was okay. Nobody was hurt. It was sort of fun coming together outside with all the people."

"Only you would think something like this is fun." I shake my head.

"I found Dad; he was okay. He and the men put together some tents and we all slept in tents. The next day we went out into the neighborhood to try to help people. Among the rubble, I saw dead bodies. People were looking for the dead and piling them in the street."

"We came back to the missionary compound to make food, then took it to the community. It was sad to see adobe houses destroyed and the rubble from the thick walls. The only thing that happened here on the property was an adobe wall that fell."

"Oh, man. I can't believe it."

"Kids were crying for their moms and couldn't find them. Some were injured or trapped under the debris. Others were dead. It was so hard."

"We didn't hear from you for three days. We were scared. We thought you might be dead. It was awful. I felt devastated at the thought that you and Dad were gone."

Devastated.

Destruction in Guatemala City, Guatemala. February 1976

Every time we move to a new city there is a familiar transition process. Say goodbye to the old school, old friends, old neighborhood, and embrace the new school, new friends and new neighborhood. And the part in the middle is the worst of it, when you feel like you are neither part of the old community nor the new. In a transition, you need to be adaptable to get through it.

However, moving to Central America was no ordinary transition because the loss was a different quality all together. After family separation and an earthquake, I felt devastated. No amount of adaptability would help. I felt a permanent loss of culture, language, traditions, and teen expectations; it was horrible.

This is what life coaches call a transformation. This is a life altering event. When something happens to you in life and it's big, like an accident, or an earthquake or a major illness, life gets categorized into before and after. Before the earthquake and after the earthquake. Before the illness and after the illness. My life can be divided into before and after devastation.

Suddenly I feel dumb. I can't speak Spanish and the culture is very different. I expected to have youth group meetings, outings with other teenagers and lots of fun in social settings. Maybe even have a boyfriend. In Guatemala, girls and boys need a chaperone if they want to date. I'm disappointed, even angry about this change.

In Guatemala, I was sick all the time. I had no best friend. Pearl was gone with her best friend and when she turned 15, she got a boyfriend. Youth group meetings are all in Spanish. I just stand there quiet because I can't express what's on my mind. I feel stupid. It feels like leaving the U.S.A. has ruined my life. And I wanted to die.

I felt lonely and over a few weeks struggled with the idea of taking my life. The one thing that kept me from this decision is that it would destroy Mom and Dad. I knew they would feel like a failure if I took my life. As much as life had been devastating, I love my family. I wouldn't want to do anything to ruin it for them.

I'm not sure how to proceed. I can be flexible and learn to live with change. But how do I adapt to devastation? How do I handle it when it's more than one devastation? I am *not* the master of my domain.

~Chapter Five~
Reader's Digest Stories

Trauma is a sucker punch to our sense of control.
Danielle Bernock[6]

As a young child, I felt hopeful and powerful. But life collided with my freedom: an earthquake, a war in the middle of Central America and sickness. Up until now, I'd lived the life I wanted but now forces greater than me were keeping me down.

The number one question I'm asked is: How are you so resilient? I didn't learn resilience from one event, one book, one sermon or one motivational quote. It's more work than that. I learned to be resilient over a period of months and years of contemplating my own survival. Practicing in my head, then practicing in real life. The big challenge for me was to stop and think because when you are an active kid like me, you have trees to climb and trails to explore. There is no time to reflect or think.

I was 12 years old when we arrived in Guatemala, which is located in the mountains. For some reason when we think of Central America, we think of beaches and palm trees, but no one tells you about their pine trees and mountains. Guatemala City is almost 5,000 feet in elevation and the elements triggered my asthma. For weeks I was sick in bed. This was torture for an active kid like me. But I found a good cure: reading. And reading can take you on an adventure of a different kind.

∽ • ∾ • ∽ • ∾

It is a low energy day, but I feel strong enough to venture outside down a tree lined dirt road to the main house. I am happy to be out of bed.

Aware of my breathing with each step, my tennis shoes crunch the pine needles. No one is around. Off in the distance I see the two-story mansion built in a contemporary architecture. It's the main house where the other missionaries live.

Maybe I'll wander by the kitchen to see if Olivia has a snack for me.

A black Labrador runs towards me, then walks beside me the rest of the way. Delighted by the company, I see he is delighted too. His tail is steadily wagging. "Okay, doggy. You have to stay outside." I step up from the grass to a concrete step and open the mansion door. The main room is huge with a small sitting area, couches and a coffee table. Immediately to my right is a simple wooden bookshelf full of books and I am drawn to them.

I pick up a little magazine and read about a family whose house suddenly fell into a sinkhole. One moment life was normal with few signs that there was trouble lurking beneath. The next moment the house was quickly flooding with water. These parents of four watched helplessly as each child drowned one-by-one. The story is both captivating and sad. I'm hooked. I flip over the small magazine in my hand. The title said *Reader's Digest*. The featured story was called "Drama in Real Life."

A disaster like that makes me think. The parents had little time to react as the disaster unfolded in minutes, maybe seconds. How would you choose which child to save? How could you move fast when life turns into slow motion? How far would you go to survive? Would you sacrifice one life for another or save yourself? How would you decide? Help the weakest? Help the one closest to you?

With these questions still in my mind, I returned to the bookshelf again and again to read more stories from "Drama in Real Life." The next story is about a man in the wilderness who was mauled by a bear. His leg was ripped open and he couldn't walk. He had to place a tourniquet on his leg to stop the bleeding. Then he willed himself to wait. He encouraged himself: "The rescue party is coming. I'm sure they are looking for me right now. Any moment now they will be here."

He became hungry and thirsty. Thirst is harder to endure, he explained. I am amazed that he expressed gratitude for what he had, if only that his heart was beating, and he was breathing. Somehow, he remained hopeful and he survived to tell the story.

In my imagination, I become the person with my leg in a tourniquet sitting there with time to think. Waiting. I imagine my butt going numb as it does when you don't move for a long time. Is life worth living if you only have one leg? As I am thinking about it, I am enduring the hardship with him, although from the comfort of a missionary home.

In my imagination, I am the hero in the wilderness, but in reality, I am the person lying in a bed too weak to walk, too weak even to eat. If I must choose between eating and breathing, I would choose to breathe.

Belinda in front of a one-room house
built by missionaries in Guatemalan villages.

During my tween years, everyone said I was bony, but I thought I was just skinny. Until one shocking day, when I took a bath and saw puddles of water forming on my pelvis. I didn't realize it then, but I read stories of survival so I could survive.

On a typical high energy day, I ran outside to see if other missionary kids were playing outside. We'd play games like hide-and-seek or volleyball or we'd swing on the rope swing. Other times we would make up our own games. My favorite was the pinecone game. We gather pines cones, scooped as many as we could in our shirts and climbed to the roof of the mansion. The access to the roof was from one of the patios. Sometimes a friend and I would carry our inconspicuous pinecones up the wide staircase and smile as adults passed. We acted sweet and nice. But on the roof, we hid from view and threw pinecones at missionaries as they walked up the path. I was always outside.

On yet another low energy day, I walked slowly to the main house. I spent the day sitting or lying in bed. However, I came to enjoy when I returned to the plain wooden bookshelf to read more survival stories. I must have read through two decades of *Reader's Digest* magazines. I sat on the floor with crossed legs, holding the small magazines with their thin shiny pages. In some stories, there were warning signs of coming trouble. Other times it was sudden disaster. They addressed a variety of topics: lost in the wilderness, lost in the desert, lost at sea, an earthquake, a kidnapping, a tsunami, a plane crash, and more. I was fascinated by the self-talk of the survivors. They repeatedly told themselves words of encouragement, "You can make it. You can do this." I admired them, especially a woman who became lost while hiking. She let herself cry for a while, then mustered herself to go on.

My heart was being challenged. Only a short time ago I felt like my life was ruined and it wasn't worth living. But here, I read stories of people who were tough. They found themselves in really tough situations—life-or-death situations—and they didn't give up. The stories called me to courage, the survivor in me began to surface.

My parents taught me that in times of crisis your character is revealed. Sometimes the people in the stories were alone, other times they had companions who complained and drained them. I wanted to be the strong character, not the one who whined or who gave up too quickly; or the one who lost hope and died. I saw it as a test of character.

These stories followed the same pattern. A person experienced a terrible accident or disaster and he or she survived. They suffered but endured the hardship. They repeatedly encouraged themselves, "You can make it. You can do this." They focused on achieving small goals despite their injuries, hunger and thirst. "Just make it for one more hour," or "Keep walking until you are over the next ridge." In the end, they developed a mantra. And just like another kid admiring the heroes, I wanted my own mantra.

In each story, the biggest challenge was internal. The survivors struggled against their thoughts and feelings. Their mind told them to stay calm; their emotions told them to panic. They had to rein in their emotions. Even though they felt like screaming hysterically or running wildly, they commanded their minds to take control.

I made several decisions about survival based on my hours and hours of reading: I wanted to survive. That became my personal mantra. Life is worth living even if I am missing a limb, an eye or whatever. My thoughts will keep me determined. Guard them. One of the bravest things I do is to face myself and change. If I don't like my first reaction, change it. Our ability to endure is very high, higher than you think it is. Life eventually returns to normal. Then it's time to do the laundry again.

In a crisis, some things are out of your control. A disaster is like a wave. You must be humble enough to know when it is time to ride the wave that you can't control. Ride it until it's over, then take control. In a way, a crisis teaches you how small you are and yet how powerful you can be. The resilience comes at the end. You take back control over your life. You don't have to be a victim, instead be a survivor.

There is something appealing about jumping up and facing a challenge, whether it's small like running out in the rain to get the clothes off the line before they get wet. Or whether it's life-threatening and you're looking down the barrel of a rifle. Human nature enjoys a good adventure. This is when you discover your power to overcome. We need challenging experiences to learn about our power.

How is it that I am resilient? Practice, practice, practice. And the work on the inside is about my thoughts and feelings. Don't ignore the feelings, but don't let them lead. Let your tough mind, your tenacity, lead you. It's the only way to survive.

You don't know how you will react until faced with a life-or-death situation. You have expectations about yourself, about the kind of person you are, or the kind of person you want to be. But when you face terror and tragedy, you find out what you're made of.

By the time we moved from Guatemala to El Salvador, I'd contemplated my death a hundred times through those stories. In a sense, I practiced how to face life-or-death situations. By the time I was 13 years old, I was even more certain. Life is worth living.

I decided that this would be the narrative I told myself: life is worth living even with hardships and suffering. I remembered Mom and Dad's words, that hardships and suffering challenge your character. It's like a sponge that is squeezed. You find out what's on the inside.

My time in Guatemala prepared me for the life-or-death moments in El Salvador. Life was pushing me to see if I was solid and immoveable. I'd say life knocked me down in Guatemala, but I learned to get up. Reading about resilience and adventures pulled out the survivor in me. Life was daring me, inviting me to do the hard work in my heart and in my mind. I never knew how important this work would be for me until later when we lived in El Salvador. How will you handle the unexpected, unexplained and unimaginable? I may have never faced down a bear in the wilderness or been stranded at sea, but my travels threw me into many life-or-death situations after our time in Guatemala.

~ Chapter Six ~
# Are We Rich?

People just want to work and provide for their family.
Noe Perez

Sometimes your lot in life is to be rich and that has one set of expectations, almost a burden. Sometimes your lot in life is to be poor and that has a different set of burdens. No matter my lot in life, I can face it if I'm together with my family.

Back in the hospital in El Salvador, I got my strength back. I was ready to return home to our light green cinder block house in our neighborhood of Scandia. On the drive home I wasn't afraid of getting shot because we weren't breaking any laws. I wasn't afraid of dying because I could breathe again.

❦ • ❧ • ❦ • ❧

In Latin America, you'll find poor people, rich people and every level in between. You'll meet people who are illiterate and those who are college educated. Some are professionals and others are laborers. The poor are poorer than the poor in the United States. And the rich here seem richer than the rich at home. Some houses have no running water. Some only have running water on a schedule. Others not only have running water all the time, but they have maids that will mix your water with fruit in a blender and bring it to you on a platter.

When we moved to El Salvador in 1977, we lived in a part of the city that had running water on a schedule. It wasn't like in the Guatemalan villages where houses have no running water. Those houses were thatched roof huts with dirt floors. And it wasn't like living in the city in Guatemala, where the house was located on a seven-acre property. The main house was a mansion that had running water all the time. We lived in Guatemala for 11 months and went back and forth between the two extremes for weeks at a time, between the humble village life and the modern city life.

Adobe house, Guatemalan village

In the villages, every morning we would see women and girls line up at one of two faucets in the entire village. Only one house in the village had electricity. Although the village was humble and many would call it poor, they were rich in another sense. Our dwelling was shabby and small. However, community life was rich. Everyone knew everyone else by name. Soon they learned our names and made us feel welcome. The people would come together for church to sing. Or they gathered to celebrate. I felt accepted and part of the community. I've moved a lot. Not every place has a strong sense of community. The villages felt safe. Pearl, Amanda and I lined up with our plastic tubs with the women. Our chore was to get water for the day and carry it the short walk home.

In El Salvador, we lived in a modern house. We had hot and cold running water (on a schedule), and electricity. This little house was better than living in the villages because it was modern. But we still had chores that involved water.

✥ • ❧ • ✥ • ❧

"Elida! I have something to show you. Call the girls," Dad says to Mom.

"Girls! Girls! Come on! Your dad has something to show us."

"Friends in the United States shipped us two metal barrels. I have them in the van. Let's see what they sent us." Soon Dad loosens a metal piece from the lip of the barrel, then pulls off the lid.

"Look. It's full of clothing," Mom says.

"And sheets." Amanda pulls out some sheets with small floral prints.

"And blankets." Pearl hands me a wool gray scratchy blanket.

In typical Mom-fashion, she snaps her fingers and points to the barrel, then the table. "Here, let's pile all of it on the dining room table. Noe, you move the barrels. One at each end of the table. Pearl, you and Amanda unload that barrel. Belinda, organize the clothes on the table in stacks by size. Come on, everyone. Many hands make for light work."

"This is fun."

"Maybe there will be something in my size."

Dad sounds excited, "I know exactly what to do with the barrels. I'm going to put them to good use. I'll place one barrel in the bathroom and another in the kitchen. We'll fill them with water so that we have a reserve when the water is shut off."

"Good idea, Noe," Mom smiles and then snaps her fingers. "Get to work."

Right next to the toilet Dad puts a plastic bucket and a barrel. "You can use the bucket to pour water into the toilet. Then the pressure makes the toilet flush."

"I didn't know you could flush a toilet that way," I say.

"Me either," Pearl shrugs her shoulders

In the following days we share the clothes and blankets.

Mom is calm in a crisis and panics over the little things. If Mom was especially panicked about the water, she would make us fill up every plastic container in the kitchen. Long rows of red bowls, blue cups and a white plastic pitcher right next to the kitchen sink on a laminated countertop. We have no kitchen cabinets above the counter and only shelves below. Across the counter are plastic bowls and pitchers of all sizes. Along the back are a row of plastic cups. Every single one is filled to the brim with water. Mom is funny.

The city operates on a rotating water schedule. When the water turns on in our neighborhood, it stays on for only about two hours. Mom runs around the house shouting, "Fill up the barrels. Fill up the barrels! HURRY! We've got water." Watching Mom panic is entertaining but watching Amanda mimic her is better. She runs into the room barefoot. "Mom says for you to come help. Fill up the barrels. Now!"

∾ • ∾ • ∾ • ∾

Mom yells, "Girls! Come on. Girls!" We gather around the dining room table in San Salvador. Dad is at the head of the table and Mom is next to him. Pearl and I are across from Mom and Amanda. Mom motions her hand to Dad as if to turn the attention to him. "Your mom and I hired a maid. Her name is Ana."

All three of us start talking at the same time.

"A maid?" Amanda asks.

"What? We are getting a maid?" Pearl asks.

"A maid, why?" I ask.

"Mommy, are we rich?" Amanda asks.

Mom motions with her hand, palm facing us, and we stop talking. Dad continues, "No, we're not rich. The maid's main job is to do laundry and cook. Washing machines are really expensive here. It's cheaper to get a maid and have her do laundry by hand."

Mom points her finger at us. "You still have to do chores. Just because Ana is here doesn't mean you don't have to work. Make your beds, set the table and clear the table every day. Every day. And don't forget to sweep and mop. Keep your rooms clean."

"Do we still have to do dishes?" Pearl and I ask at the same time. We look at each other, smile and bump elbows.

Mom and Dad answer at the same time, "Yes." That's a firm yes.

Never in a million years would I expect that we would have a maid. I thought only rich people had maids. It's hard to understand my place in society. One moment I'm walking to the local faucet to get water for the day. Next moment I'm living in a modern house. And then another time, I'm visiting friends in El Salvador who have several maids. We swim in their pool and a maid brings us shakes. Am I privileged? Sometimes. But I have mixed feelings living in a house that sometimes has running water which seems humbling. But it's the same house where we get a maid. Life is confusing.

Mom says, "She's coming this afternoon. You be nice to her." She looks directly at Pearl, "No jokes. I'm serious." Pearl laughs nervously and gets a gleam in her eye; she's so funny. Mom points her finger at Pearl, and she wipes the smirk off her face.

Family meetings happen in one of two places, on Mom and Dad's bed or at the dining room table.

On this particular afternoon, Mom yells for us to come to the table. "Girls! Come on. Girls!"

Mom sits at the head of the dining room table and an older girl sits next to her. Pearl and I sit next to each other and Amanda is next to the new girl.

Mom says in Spanish, "Let me introduce you to Ana." Mom points to Pearl, Amanda and me as she says our names and we smile on cue. "This is Pearl, the oldest. This is Belinda, the middle girl. And this is Amanda, the youngest."

Ana is 17 years old, only four years older than me. She stood a little over five feet tall and looked as if she didn't even weigh 100 pounds. She has black, wavy hair, dark eyes and tan skin. She looks like us.

Mom explains in Spanish. "Ana. The girls will do their chores. You'll cook and do laundry. I'm telling you in front of the girls so that they don't tell you any different." Ana's eyebrows raise slightly. She doesn't say anything. Now we can't ask Ana to do stuff for us. There's no getting around the rules with Mom. She gets up from the table and invites Ana to follow her. "Let me show you your room and the kitchen."

The average home in our neighborhood has live-in maids. They cook, clean, provide childcare and do the laundry. The average pay is $20.00 per month with room and board. (Note that minimum wage in the U.S. was $2.30 per hour.) Young girls who don't get an education or vocational training often become maids. The government provides for basic education up to the eighth grade. Families are required to pay for high school and college education. These are luxuries for the privileged. I remember seeing teenagers dressed in school uniforms lining up at a bus stop. I thought they were dorks, but here the uniform is a symbol of status and privilege.

I wonder about Ana. Did she grow up in the country? Was her house a small hut with dirt floors? Did she have electricity and running water in her house? Did she miss home?

⋄ • ⋄ • ⋄ • ⋄

At dinnertime Mom invites Ana to sit at the table. She looks uncomfortable. We eat as Mom speaks in Spanish to include Ana. This is hard for me. My Spanish isn't very good, and Pearl makes fun of me. Ana serves herself last. She doesn't say anything the entire time. She just looks down at her food, hesitates and then eats.

Amanda gets up and starts making piles of dishes to carry to the kitchen. She returns with a wet cloth to wipe it clean. Pearl and I stand at the sink and watch the suds grow like a little mountain of temptation. The suds call us to play with them. Ana walks just as Pearl taps my chin with a swoosh of suds. The fights are always gentle with Pearl placing suds on my head and us both giggling. Then it's my turn to get her with suds, and we giggle more. We both have suds in our hair and Pearl reaches over and puts a beard of suds on my chin. We stop when Ana enters. She looks at us and raises her eyebrows. She doesn't say anything. When she leaves, we continue our playful fight.

I talk to Mom later. "Mom. Ana seems uncomfortable. I worry about her."

Mom smiles. "She'll warm up. Give her time."

I keep thinking and hesitating, but then I say, "She seems closed off. What happened to her?"

Mom touches my arm gently. "I don't know, mija. Give her time with us and she'll open up."

I love it when Mom calls me mija.

◈ • ◈ • ◈ • ◈

I'm a thinker. I have a lot of questions about God and life. Maybe this explains why I have such a fond connection with my journal. I love to have time alone to reflect. I even think about Santa Claus. When I was five years old, I learned that Santa Claus was not a real person. I was so sad, not because of gifts but because he was good. Already, I knew about war because my dad was fighting in Vietnam. Every day the news talked about the men dying in the war. When I learned that Santa was not real, my only thought was that there is no genuinely good person on earth. These days I'm thinking a lot about suffering and war.

Even now when I think back to that cinder-block house in El Salvador, one of the most prominent memories involves the water situation because of how it made me feel. When water shuts off, life stops. Everything else is put aside because you can't live without it.

When Mom and Dad are doing errands in the city, it is our responsibility to fill up the barrels. It makes me feel important.

When Mom and Dad come home, it is crazy when the water comes on.

Mom runs through the house screaming, in English, "Water! Turn on the water!" I can only imagine what Ana thinks when she sees this chubby Mexican American woman with curly black hair running barefoot through the house. That's Mom in a panic. I laugh at Mom because of the way she panics about the water. Mostly, I laugh because she runs through the house screaming like a crazy woman.

That's the first time we see Ana laugh. She raises her hands to cover her mouth. Ana usually walks with her shoulders slightly tense. This is the first time I see her loosen up. She doesn't laugh out loud, but you can see her eyes smiling.

All three of us girls run through the house to turn on the faucets.

"The water is on in the bathroom!" Pearl shouts.

"I got the water on in the kitchen," I shout back. Our assignment is to keep an eye on the barrels until they are full.

I could barely hear Amanda who was outside by the *pila*, which is Spanish for wash basin."

There is something magical when life stops. For a moment, the heaviness of life lifts. One moment everyone is in different parts of the house being responsible: doing homework, reading or working. The next moment we drop everything and come together. It's fun. I love the coming-together feeling. If I shout out to my family, they stop everything and come running. It makes me smile. I feel part of something that's bigger than me.

In El Salvador, we are in this together. After everything settles down, I stand at the bathroom sink. With water running over my hands, I pray, "Thank you, God, for water."

You only appreciate it when you don't have it.

"Thank you, God.

Thank you.

Thank you.

Thank you."

~Chapter Seven~
Sometimes You Fight

Keep the peace, but sometimes you fight.

Noe Perez

Back in El Salvador in 1977. Ana and Amanda walk in the front door with a stack of tortillas wrapped in a towel. The metal security door slams with a loud crash.

My little sister, Amanda, shrugs. "Oops. The wind caught the door, and my hands are full. I didn't mean to slam the door." She's eight years old and dressed in a matching summer top and shorts with little strawberries. Ana is from El Salvador. She cooks and does the wash for us. Amanda loves to spend time with Ana doing the washing and chores.

Every neighborhood has a tortilla lady. You recognize her house because of the long line of people waiting outside her door. The tortilla lady grinds the corn fresh every day and cooks the tortillas over an open fire. They're thick, round, about four inches in diameter and delicious.

Pearl pulls out a gray metal folding chair to sit at the dining room table. "Mom, I love the new tablecloth you bought. It's so colorful." She touches the area in front of her with her hands.

"We need something to brighten up …" Mom looks around the room at the lonely white walls.

Ana places a plastic plate in front of me with a stack of tortillas and a whole avocado. Steam drifts up from the tortillas. I squeeze the avocado and it's nice and soft, just right. This dinner is my favorite: corn tortillas and avocados.

Dad clears his throat. "I know we got broken into recently. I talked to the Lopez family about it." We're all busy leaning over our plates eating. Dad's words are deliberate with pauses between the words. "In El Salvador every house has a dog and a gun."

Pearl, Amanda and I stop eating and look at Dad.

"Are we getting a dog?" I blurt out with food in my mouth.

Without a word, Mom's disapproving eyes said, "Belinda! Cover your mouth."

Amanda swallows fast. "Are we getting a dog?"

In the silence no one moves or chews. All eyes are on Dad. "Yes, we are getting a dog."

In a burst of joy, Pearl, Amanda and I squeal in unison. "We're getting a dog! We're getting a dog!"

Dad clears his throat. "In fact, the Lopez's German Shepherd is having a litter soon. They promised to give me one." Dad looks to Mom. "And they said they will get us a gun if we want one."

All three girls talk at the same time. Ana looks curiously at us from behind her long bangs.

We turn to one another, "We need a name for the dog. What's a good dog name?"

Amanda jumped up. "Maximillian."

I say, "That's too long. We need something shorter."

Pearl thought, "Spot. No, too common. Rufus, too fluffy."

Amanda suggests, "McMillan, like the show, McMillan and Wife."

Pearl complains, "No, still too long. How about Mac which is short for McMillan?"

Amanda with Mac
(3 months old)

I'm so excited about the dog, I couldn't care less about a gun.

When I was seven years old, Dad taught me to fight. When he was in school a group of boys in his neighborhood harassed him. Day after day, the same group hassled and wore him down.

Dad warned them to back off or he would hurt them. They should have listened because when Dad had had enough, he beat up all of them. They never bothered him again. Dad was firm about his beliefs. You keep the peace, but sometimes you fight.

"There's more," Dad interrupts. We stop talking. "Second of all, they said, robbers will target the house if it's empty. So, we can't all go out together all the time. We need someone to stay here at the house. Thirdly, we need to decide if we want a gun. I'm not sure I want one."

Mom raises her hands like she's leading a choir. "I can see it now, the newspaper headlines in bold print: 'Missionary Kills Robber.' Not a good idea. We came here to bring people good news. It wouldn't be good if…"

"I think we need to pray about this. It's a big decision to get a gun. First of all, it's my job to protect my family. If someone breaks into our house, I have no problem hurting them. Did you know that if you put three pounds of pressure on someone's knee, it will break? That's all it takes is three pounds of pressure. If you're ever in a situation where you are on the ground and someone is standing over you, you have the advantage. You can use your legs to break their knee. Your legs have the strongest muscles in your body. Girls, you remember that, if you're in a situation where you must defend yourself," Dad nods.

"I know our house has been broken into two times, but I don't know…" Mom is thinking out loud.

Mom snaps her fingers. "Ah, I get it. We're from the United States of America. They think we have money." Mom laughs.

It seems funny to me. People are trying to steal from missionaries. We arrived in this country with one suitcase each. We have furniture made by my dad. He learned a lot from his carpenter dad. He made the beds we sleep in. We don't even own a television, not for religious reasons but because we can't afford one.

"Still we need to protect our family. Girls. Make sure we keep the doors locked." Dad is firm.

Dad believes in protecting family at all costs. Sometimes you must fight to protect your family. Sometimes you have to fight to protect yourself. Sometimes you have to go to war. Violence is an option, but it's always a last resort. It's interesting to hear him talk about getting a gun. He's trained in how to use one.

I stay there eating my corn tortilla and savoring the avocado. "Mm um." What would it be like to have a gun?

Mom is thinking. "You know, we didn't come here to get involved in politics. And we certainly didn't come here to hurt people. I know people might break into our house…"

Dad points out, "We came to bring people good news. We didn't come to kill people, even if they are trying to harm us."

Dad continues eating and thinking. "I'm going to ask God to give us wisdom about this. I want to protect my family. But I don't know about getting a gun."

"How can this help? If we kill someone who is breaking in our house, how is this going to help us build a church? How can this be good?"

Should we have a gun? I don't know. I would feel awful having to kill somebody. And really, I don't care about all that. I just want a dog.

※ • ※ • ※ • ※

At breakfast the next day, I smell hot coffee and hear the clinking of spoons on mugs. In the middle of the table is a plate of pan dulce, sweet bread in Spanish. They're like donuts from the States, but not as sweet. This is a treat.

I pour myself a cup of milk and look for a chocolate concha. The topping crumbles with each bite, but I don't care that I am leaving a little pile of crumbs on the table. Oh, its soft. This is fresh.

Amanda begs, "Can I have coffee?"

"Coffee is for adults. You're still growing." Mom points to the milk carton. "Drink your milk."

Amanda sits in the chair next to me with a pouty lip and reaches for an empanada. It's like an apple turnover but with pumpkin inside. She reaches for the milk in slow motion. You can see her sadness in the movement.

Dad sips his coffee and clears his throat. "We've prayed about it and we don't want to get a gun. We came here to help. We're going to trust God to protect us. I know there's a chance that one of us will get killed because of all the violence in this country. But we're going to leave that in God's hands. When I was in Vietnam, men died right next to me, on one side and on the other. I thought, if God wants me to live, he's going to have to keep me alive. That's my thought here. If God wants us to live, he'll have to keep us alive. In fact, if God wants us to live, there is no one who can stop him."

Mom and Dad have a simple faith. They aren't in denial about the dangers. They trust God with our lives as well as our deaths. This is surrender. Mom and Dad surrendered their life to God. They believed that whether you live or die, you do it for the Lord. I don't know if that is what I believe.

෴ • ෴ • ෴ • ෴

A few days later, Ana shares a story with us. It's the first time she said more than just a few words. We're at breakfast around the table, each eating our cereal and milk. Mom and Dad have their coffee. Ana says, in Spanish, "Someone tried to break into the house last night."

Pearl, Amanda and I look up from our bowls. Mom and Dad look at each other with concern and wide eyes. We stop eating and every head turns toward Ana.

"What? What happened?" Mom asks.

Ana shifts in her seat. "I heard a noise and saw the shadow of a man in the back patio. I was scared. I wanted to get something to protect myself, but suddenly there was a gust of wind that slammed the door. The man ran off."

Mom is a storyteller. When missionaries visit us in the next few weeks, Mom shares Ana's story. "We got broken into three times in the first few weeks of living here." She smiles. "The funny thing is that the third time they came at night. And Ana heard someone in the back patio. Just then a gust of wind caught the metal door between the carport and the back patio, and the door slammed with a loud noise. It sounded like a gun, so the robbers ran off."

We laugh. The missionaries look at us. They don't see the humor. Mom explains, "We debated whether or not we should get a gun. We asked God for wisdom. We decided not to buy one but to trust God to protect us. Then, the next time robbers come to our house, the door slams and it sounds like a gun and they run away."

The neighbors think we have a gun. I think God has a sense of humor.

~ Chapter Eight ~
# Passport Stamps and Twinkies

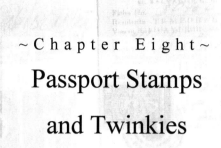

I'm so gorgeous. I don't know what to do with myself.
Elida Perez

If only 42% of U.S. citizens have passports, that means the majority the people in the U.S.A. don't have first-hand experience with travel that involves immigration.[7]

In November 1977, we moved downtown to a neighborhood called Isidro Menendez. Within walking distance from our four-bedroom townhouse was a café, a large hospital and a traffic circle with a water fountain. Plenty of shops and restaurants dotted the four-lane highway. The U.S. American Embassy, which takes up an entire city block, was a few blocks away. The embassy was like a fortress surrounded with a hedge of bushes and heavy metal fencing. We were now in the city with bustling city streets, but ours was a quiet street with a tight row of two-story townhomes. We discovered that if you lived close to a hospital, you would have running water all the time.

El Salvador immigration required our sponsoring organization to be recognized by the government. This required paperwork which kept Dad busy. Once it was done, Mom and Dad became residents of El Salvador at no fee. They only had to pay $800.00 each for us three girls.

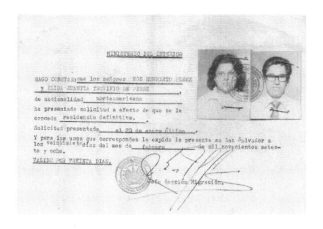

From the upstairs bathroom Mom sticks her head out the door. "Come on, we need to leave in 15 minutes. Hurry up."

I lean on the doorjamb of the bathroom. "I still need to brush my teeth."

Mom looks at herself in the mirror, leans forward as she scrunches her curly hair. "I'm so gorgeous. I don't know what to do with myself." As she exits and points a finger at me, "Hurry up."

"Yes, ma'am." Mom cracks me up.

We rush about because of immigration. Our official status in El Salvador is tourists which allows us to stay in the country for 90 days at a time. When we become residents, we are welcome to stay for a year. Every 90 days we travel to Guatemala City to get a new tourist stamp on our navy-blue passports. This extra travel isn't all bad because Mom and Dad attend missionary meetings in Guatemala, and we get our school supplies from the CAG. The trips are a hassle except I use the time to read.

Mom yells, "Come on! We're going to Guatemala. Let's go! Move it, move it." I hear the pad of bare feet on the cool tile. We run to the van with shoes in one hand and carry-on bags in the other. All three of us pile into the van for the five-hour trip. We slam the door of the van while it's moving. I feel rushed.

"Belinda, when we get to the border make sure to tell them that you were born in the United States," Mom pleads.

Everyone in my family was born in the United States of America except me. I was born on an American military base in Germany. Mom, Dad and Amanda were all born in Texas. Pearl was born in Arizona.

It's the only time my parents ever ask me to lie. It's a technicality. Yes, I am a citizen of the United States of America. No, I was not born in the United States of America. Yes, I was born on a military base in Germany, which is like U.S. American soil but is not, technically.

As we drive out of the city, I'm thinking. What do I do with present circumstances? If I lie, the border crossing goes smoother. If I tell the truth and say I'm born in Germany, Dad must explain that he was in the U.S. military. That's why I was born in Germany. Then he must convince the officials that he is no longer in the army.

If I lie, I'm not the person I want to be. I'll disappoint myself. Dad teaches us a lot about being a person of integrity. I want to be that kind of person. If I tell the truth, it puts my family in danger. The officers must decide whether we are a military threat. I can't lie. Besides, if they look at my passport closely, they'll see that I was born in Germany.

Our border crossings experiences have been unpredictable. Some officers are kind and make the process smooth and quick. They're pleasant when they look at our passports and stamp them.

Other soldiers create a tense, hostile environment. They make us wait with smirks on their faces.

Mom turns around from her seat up front. "I have a great idea. When we get to the border, we'll befriend the officers. Noe, you take all the passports from office to office to gather stamps and pay the fees. While he is inside, I'll talk to the officers on the Guatemala side. Pearl, you go talk to the officers on the El Salvador side. Amanda, you stick around the van to see if you can make friends with the suitcase inspector. Belinda, you … um. You stick close to the van and keep an eye on your sister. Everyone has a job to do. Do it. If it goes like I expect it to, the officers will go easy on us."

My Spanish isn't good, so my job is to guard the van. If I open my mouth, everyone will know I am a foreigner.

We all have tan skin and dark hair, and we blend in. All except Mom. She has fair skin, dark hair and Hispanic facial features.

Mom and Dad's first language is Spanish. Pearl, Amanda and I started learning Spanish when we arrived in Guatemala. I am the worst at it. I got so tired of people laughing at my terrible Spanish that I stopped talking. It was too embarrassing. I understand Spanish, but when it comes to talking, I can't seem to find the words. When I pronounce words wrong, I wind up staying something that I don't mean. When I speak Spanish, I feel a big neon sign pointing to me that says, "Gringa here! Gringa here!" And Pearl laughs at me.

Amanda is the best with Spanish. She was seven years old when we moved to Central America. If you learn a language before the age of eight, you are more likely to speak like a native. If you learn a second language after the age of eight, there is a good chance you will speak it with an accent. Always.

People are attracted to Pearl. She is so beautiful. But more than that, she is good at listening to people and has a beautiful spirit. I walk around the van and see her smiling at a soldier. He smiles back. Yeah, she's got his attention.

After guarding the van for about 30 minutes, an officer approaches me. This is the moment I dread, and my stomach gets tense. Instead of asking each one of us where we were born, he asks, "Are you a U.S. American citizen?" I feel relieved and gladly say "Yes" because it's true.

Amanda hangs around close to the van. She is supposed to befriend the officer who inspects the van and our suitcases. He usually hangs around outside. If Amanda charms the officer, he might not even open the suitcases. Amanda makes people laugh.

He might look at Amanda and say, "Oh, this is your family? That's okay. Just get going." He is the last official we must see before we start this process all over again on the Guatemalan side.

I get afraid at the border, not because we have done anything illegal. I feel afraid because the people in uniform have the power to detain us. They can revoke our right to be here. They have the power, and we are subject to their moods and whims.

∽ • ∾ • ∽ • ∾

My parents were part of an organization called Christians in Action. We playfully called it CIA. Not *The CIA*, but just CIA. After we arrived in El Salvador, we stopped using the CIA-joke. We called it CinA for short. We couldn't risk being misunderstood. CinA was composed of people with different theologies and politics: Baptists, Methodists, Presbyterians, and other. Some were Democrats, others Republican. This made for interesting conversations with other missionaries.

My life was rich with adventure. I appreciated my parents especially when I reflected on our stories. Since other missionaries also had to travel to the border to get their passports stamped, we had many guests at our house from the U.S. and other countries: Montana, California, Texas, Puerto Rico, Canada, and Colombia. What I saw was people united in their hearts and not divided by ideology. They had many conversations about the heart. The missionary, you see, is part humanitarian and part evangelical. They build houses and distribute clothes and medical supplies. They pray for people and tell them about Jesus.

≪ • ≫ • ≪ • ≫

In El Salvador, the living room has a simple mid-century couch. When a group of missionaries visit, we set up folding chairs in a circle. Imagine a passionate and idealistic group of 20- and 30-year-olds: tall missionary, bald missionary, always dieting missionary, hometown missionary, urban missionary. Men, women, couples, singles; all were represented.

Tall missionary asks, "Are you feeding a corrupt system if you bribe a government official?"

Bald missionary responds. "Another question. Are you letting them waste your time? If you don't bribe them, the whole border process takes longer. It saves time if you bribe them and we have more important things to do."

"But it just feels wrong to give a bribe," says Always Dieting missionary.

"We're here to learn about their culture. This is how their culture works. Don't we have to adapt?" Canadian missionary adjusts her glasses.

Dad objects. "What about setting a positive example?" He never tried to bribe an official. He's follows the rules strictly and refuses to pay bribes.

"Really, I can't do something that is against my conscience," Puerto Rican missionary says.

"Well, we wouldn't want you to do that," says Urban missionary.

My mom says, "You have to follow your heart. What's right for …"

"Yes, each person decides for themselves, and I have no problem handing out a little money here and there. It doesn't bother me one bit." Bald missionary sits back confidently in his seat.

And on and on they explore the topic of bribery at the border. And all I hear is a group of people who have sacrificed much in order to be here. They're each trying to figure out a way to live out their faith in a way that doesn't violate their hearts. I love it.

Always dieting missionary says, "We were approached at the border by some soldiers in uniform. When they walked to our car I was really afraid because they had rifles with them. I didn't know what they would do to us. One leaned down and, through my car window, said, 'Elvis died today.' Here, I'm expecting something scary and he tells me about Elvis. It was so funny!"

Mom shares a story about one of their trips. "Noe and I drove to the El Salvador border without the girls. About 10 miles before we got to the border, we saw three soldiers walking along the side of the road. Just some young guys. They had rifles and were waving their arms for us to stop.

"I turned to Noe and said, 'Don't stop.' But you know Noe. He always does the right thing."

"He said to me, 'I have to stop. They are waving us down.'"

She continues. "Noe pulled over to the side of the road. They came up to my window."

"One of them asked for a ride to the border. So, I asked them, 'Are you good people? We only give rides to good people.'"

"They replied, 'Oh yes, Ma'am. We're good people.' All three of them talked at the same time nervously. So, Noe let them ride with us to the border!"

Mom finished her story. "Your Dad started telling them the story of Jesus." My mom is outrageous and my dad so steady and reliable.

Laughter echoes on the cinder block walls from around the circle.

❦ • ❧ • ❦ • ❧

One of our border crossings was particularly scary.

Amanda climbs to the top of the stairs, puts her hands on her hips, and says, "Mom says to pack. We are leaving for Guatemala."

During our drive to the border, I am reading a book for school, *Hansi: The Girl Who Loved the Swastika* by Maria Anne Hirchmann. The book describes how Hansi, who was part of Nazi Youth, became a Christian. Her story is about her relationship with God and all that she suffered. She was arrested and sent to prison because she was a Christian.

What would it be like to be incarcerated for your faith? What would it be like to die for your faith? Will someone in my family have to die? Will I? When we arrive at the El Salvador border, I forget to put my book away. It's in plain sight.

I look up and see a building with a long, shaded area like a gas station but there are no gas pumps. We pull into the parking bay.

Dad grabs the stack of passports.

"I'll be right back."

The rest of us split up to make friends with the border officers again. Pearl talks to the El Salvador officer. Mom talks to Guatemalan officer. Amanda and I are near the van. She is looking for the officer who inspects the van. Dad walks from office to office to process our passports. I hope this doesn't take too long.

I walk around the van and keep an eye on Amanda as she talks to the officer. Dad returns with our passports and approaches the officer talking to Amanda. She introduces the officer in Spanish, saying, "I present you to my father, Noe Perez."

They shake hands and exchange pleasantries.

Dad hands him our passports, the officer smiles as he examines them.

They approach the van. The officer asks to see our luggage. We open the back of the van, and I see it. Beyond the suitcases my book is lying on the seat. A large Nazi Swastika is printed on the cover. The officer looks through the suitcases and then he sees the book. Dad sees it too and he starts talking fast. He explains that the book is a testimony about how the young girl was touched by God. (Its not an actual handbook on how to be a Nazi.) The officer has a stern look on his face. He asks Dad to unload the suitcases.

The government official opens each suitcase and holds up each item. He searches through each pocket. In my suitcase, he rifles through my clothes, my Bible and my journal. That's when I realize that a soldier can read my journal if he thinks he should. They're watching us.

The officer is not smiling anymore. He turns to Dad and says, "Come with me."

Oh boy. Waiting is so hard because my imagination goes wild. What will happen now? What did I do? Are we going to get into trouble? Will we be arrested? I sit in the van and pray for protection over me and my family.

Time goes by slowly. Mom and Pearl return to the van and I tell them what happened.

Then Dad returns with our passports in hand. I don't know what Dad said to the official, but I am so happy when we get back on the road. And I am not surprised to hear Dad tell me to put a cover on my book. I should have known better than to leave my book lying around. I was careless. I could hear Dad's anger in his tone of voice. I don't blame him. I put the family in danger. That was a close call.

I hide my book in my suitcase. The border crossing at Guatemala goes smooth. We get on the road again and Mom says, "Let's play a game." She is good at relieving the tension. She asks a question. "If you could have anything from the United States, right now, what would you choose?" We played this game often because we missed home so much. And we need to shift the atmosphere away from our close call.

As always, Amanda says, "I want peanut butter! The kind from the States. Skippy."

I said, "I want a candy bar, maybe a Snickers bar or a Hershey bar. Anything chocolate, but preferably a Snickers bar."

Pearl says, "Hm. I want the big bubble gum. Hubba Bubba."

Mom says, "I want a big juicy Whataburger with French fries and a Pepsi. Okay, Noe, what do you want?" And we wait for Dad to speak.

Dad says, "I want a Twinkie."

I say, "Yum, that sounds good. I want a Twinkie too."

We come around a small hill and the timing could not be more perfect. Right in front of us is a huge billboard on the side of the road announcing that Twinkies are coming to Guatemala. We laugh and start talking at the same time.

"I want a Twinkie."

"I want one too."

In a chorus, all at once, we say, "Me too." We laugh as we drive down the road.

Mom says, "You know, nobody would believe us if we told them our stories."

Immediately we go off in search of Twinkies.

~ Chapter Nine ~

Hiding in the Theater

I lost my peace. I need to go back and find it.

Noe Perez

In our days of escalating turmoil, people need a way to find strength. I didn't find strength by pursuing strength. I found strength by pursuing peace.

What is it like when God speaks? Does he have a deep voice? Is there a choir singing in the background? Does the voice come down from the sky? Do the clouds part with sunlight shining down? Does he shout? Is he angry? Is he impatient, cruel or demanding?

Everyone at church talks about hearing his voice. I doubt them. What if they say God told them something just to get what they want? People can be dishonest.

I was 10 years old when I got my first journal. At church they were encouraging everyone to use a journal to track one's spiritual growth. It is not a diary. Let me be clear about that. Keeping a diary is silly to me. It's something that girly girls do; and I'm not a girly girl. I don't like makeup, curlers and dolls. I like skateboards and climbing trees. I got a journal, but I told myself it is completely different than a diary.

The church taught me this practice. Say a simple prayer, "God, what would you like to say to me today?" While I sit silently in front of my open journal, I read my Bible. I'm centering my life around God by stopping twice a day to focus on him and listen for what he says. I write down today's date and anything that floats into my head. Even if I'm not sure it's from God.

At first this was hard for me. I was only 10 years old and the Bible had a lot of big words. I didn't like to stop reading just to look up words in a dictionary. I decided to ignore the words I didn't understand and pay attention to those I did.

This was also hard because I didn't know what it was like to "hear from God." I wish I had started my reading with the story of Elijah. When he was learning to hear from God, Elijah expected God to speak to him in an earthquake or in lightening. But God spoke to him in a still, small voice. I don't know what I expected, perhaps something audible. For sure, I thought God would speak in a louder voice, maybe not an earthquake or lightening. But I didn't expect him to use a quiet voice. After about three months of practicing devotions, I started hearing God speak to me.

How do you describe something that is spirit? It's hard to find the words for something that is real but not material. I'm learning about hearing from God. It's not a voice. It's a thought that floats in your head. Not your own thought. It's not something I touch, see, or hear audibly. I feel it in my heart or spirit, but not like an emotional feeling. It's a spiritual feeling, like an impression.

I like to write down what I hear, but I doubt myself. Did I hear that right? Are these God's thoughts or my own thoughts?

༄ • ༅ • ༄ • ༅

I hate the shootouts. I stand in the driveway of our house and listen for gunfire from downtown. If I am very quiet, I can hear the soldiers and rebels shooting at each other from far away. I hear the steady hum of traffic, but no shots. I look up to the sky for helicopters because sometimes soldiers shoot at people from above. I don't see any. I report back to Dad.

"All clear," I call.

Mom yells, "Let's go. Move it. Move it!"

Pearl and Amanda run downstairs, crashing into each other as they race to the van. We know we only have a few minutes to get into the van before Mom will leave us behind. She is not a patient person. She *will* leave us behind.

It's really not fair for Amanda when we race. Pearl is seven years older and I'm five years older that Amanda. Pearl beats Amanda to the van. She stands there leaning forward on her tiptoes, gloating. Dad pauses in the driveway and listens. It's quiet. We pile into our van for the trip downtown.

As usual Mom is talking, and Dad is listening as he drives. I look out the window at the trees, enjoying the sunny weather. The windows are open and warm air touches my face and gently moves my long hair around.

Normally we go straight to the post office, but today we turn the corner into an unfamiliar part of the city. There are no spaces between the buildings, making the street feel crowded. There are no trees to admire here, only two-story buildings that are built right up to the sidewalk.

Then I hear it. Gunshots. Mom stops in mid-sentence. No one says a word. Pearl, Amanda and I drop to the floor of the van. Dad finds an empty parking space in a nearly full lot. This is good because we can hide between the cars. The blunt sounds of gunfire are coming from down the street.

I start reviewing Dad's instructions in my head. When you hear gunfire: Hide. Don't look to see what is happening! Be quiet, sit still and listen. Don't give away your position. Watch me and do what I say. Don't ask questions; just do what I say.

Dad has trained us for dangerous moments like these. He said, "I need your unquestioning obedience. If you stand there asking for an explanation, it puts us all in danger. You can always ask questions later when we are home safe. Just do what I say! Don't hesitate."

If we hesitate, it could be a disaster.

I remember when Dad made us run drills.

"Duck!"

We all dove to the floor. Dad smiled, "That was good. Get up. Now, hide!" Pearl, Amanda and I ran up the stairs to hide in closets. He trained us for moments like these and here we are.

A tall red brick wall stands along one side of the parking lot. It provides good cover. Across the street is a movie theater.

One by one we get out of the van and crouch down, hiding between the parked cars. I try to be still like a statue, so I don't give away our position. I look to Dad to see what he wants us to do. I'm expecting some kind of hand signal. Dad looks calm. He doesn't often show his emotions. I wouldn't know if he felt panic or relief. He has a tense look on face. This is serious.

I force myself to be quiet and motionless. No jerking movements. No screaming or running away. It is hard to not move when your gut is screaming at you to run away. Dad trained us. Your mind tells your body what to do.

I see Dad hide between two cars that are parked on the street. He squats between the cars and steadies himself with a hand on each bumper. I follow him, darting from car to car. I squat in a small spot between the cars, and steady myself like Dad. Pearl is near me. Amanda is holding hands with Mom. All of us are crouching in this small space.

My heart beats wildly. I focus on Dad. I am aware of every movement, every moment. My eyes bounce back and forth from one family member to another. Everything else moves in slow motion. I'm checking to see that Dad, Pearl, Amanda and Mom are still unharmed. The next few minutes could change my life forever if I lose somebody I love. My body is tense as the gravity of our situation weighs on me.

The street is empty. The only thing I hear is gunfire. Rat-a-tat-tat. Rat-a-tat-tat. Rat-a-tat-tat. My heart pounds so loud I hear it in my ears. The street is empty from people. They are all hiding. The most dangerous part right now is crossing the street.

Who would think that such a simple task could be a huge challenge? Cross the street and walk into a theater, that's all. That is simple, really. Look both ways and cross the street. You do it a thousand times and don't think about it.

We move in a single file. Dad is in front; Mom is behind. Mom and Dad planned ahead. If we walk down a street, one walks in front and the other in back. Then if one of them gets killed, their girls still have one surviving parent.

Dad signals with his hands. Get down low.

With his palm, he says, "Wait."

He waves his hand. "Come slowly."

Palm up. "Wait."

Hand wave. "Come."

Dad crosses the street and slips into the theater. Dad is safe. He stands behind the closed door, but I see him open it slightly so he can signal to us.

Pearl runs across the street as fast as lightening. She is safe.

I pause between the same two cars. I peek out slightly to look down the street toward the gunfire. My anxiety peaks for a minute. I listen for cars. Then I dart across the street as if I'm running the most important race in my life. I slam into Dad. He receives me gladly. I am safe.

He signals Mom and Amanda, palm up. "Wait." Then waves his hand to come. They slip in past the door. Mom and Amanda are safe.

"Are you okay?" Mom says.

"Yeah, I'm okay," I respond.

Mom turns to Pearl, "Are you okay?"

Pearl says, "I'm okay."

Mom says to Dad, "Are you okay?" He nods.

Mom turns to Amanda who is still holding her hand, "Are you okay, mija?"

Amanda looks up at Mom and wrinkles her nose. "Yeah, I'm okay. Daddy, are we going to watch a movie?"

Mom and Dad look at each other and nod. We all breathe a sigh of relief. I straighten my shoulders and walk to the glass ticket counter. All kinds of candies are on display. I act normal, but my heart is still pounding in my chest. I know that it will calm down eventually. This happens all the time, but it always fades. Then I pick up where I left off: homework, chores, laundry. Today, it's a movie.

Being missionaries, my parents are conservative with their money and even more conservative about movies. We run into a theater to escape a shootout. Mom and Dad select a kid-friendly baseball movie: *The Bad News Bears Go to Japan.* We know we can't go wrong with a baseball movie. We haven't heard anything about the other movie in the double feature: *Jaws.* If it's showing with the kid movie, it should be fun too.

Mom and Dad let each of us pick two lollypops. At the ticket counter, I select my favorite flavors: cherry and grape. When we enter the auditorium, people are sitting everywhere. I am amazed that everyone acts normal. Then I realize that I am acting normal too.

As we look for seats, the auditorium is already dark. We sit in the same order that we entered: Dad, Pearl, me, Amanda and Mom. The theater seats are large and comfortable.

The movie starts with ominous drumming music. I am captivated by the movie *Jaws.* We don't know it's a scary movie. But for a couple of hours, I'm afraid of sharks instead of gunfire. It is strange kind of relief.

As the lights come up, I turn to Pearl, "So what did you think?"

She exclaims, "I loved it!"

My beautiful sister Pearl starts describing her favorite parts. I hold my two lollypop sticks close to my mouth and fiddle with them, listening to her.

Then I interrupt her, "Where are your lollypop sticks?"

Looking around, she gasps and sinks deep into her chair. Slowly she says, "I think I ate them!" We lean in towards each other and giggle.

"I was so wrapped up in the movie and anxious that I didn't notice I was nibbling on them!"

I tell Dad and Amanda about the missing lollypop sticks. We all laugh.

When Mom returns from the bathroom, we tell her about Pearl's sticks. We all roar with laughter.

What else is there to do when your life has just flashed before your eyes, except to laugh? Mom gasps and says, "We are going to get killed in this shootout. The newspaper headline will read: Missionaries Shot in Movie Theater."

Mom's concern is genuine. Yet somehow, all the tension and anxiety is released into the air when we laugh.

Mom laughs at herself and points her finger at us. "In times like this, we either laugh or cry. I'd rather laugh."

And we did laugh, often. I can't remember what happened when we left the theater. All I know is that somehow, we made it home after the second movie.

❧ • ❧ • ❧ • ❧

I settle on my bed and get comfortable on my stomach. My heart is calm now. My journal is open in front of me. I bend my knees and my feet rock back and forth behind me. I flip to an empty page in my blue journal. I write the date and the passage that I am reading.

I'm the kind of person who doesn't know who to trust. I don't always take people at their word. I want to see for myself. The whole point of being able to hear God's determines whether or not I trust the source. If God moves my spirit and speaks to me through a book or translation or sermon, I accept it as valid.

I never heard God in an audible voice, but I felt his stirrings in whispers and nudges. When I read the Bible, a phrase or word stands out to me. In my spirit, it jumps off the page and hovers above it, and then suddenly it's gone. Like I see arrows pointing to it. Or it's God pointing it out. Highlighter, emphasis, nudge, arrows. I don't know how to explain it. God is pointing to something, like he is saying, "Pay attention. I'm trying to speak to you."

I start with a question: "God, what is it that you want to say to me?" I read and I listen. If anything—a word, a phrase, a verse—is highlighted, I write it in my journal.

My goal at this point is not to study the Bible so I can know more. Instead I'm making a spiritual connection to my maker. I need encouraging and powerful words that shine light into darkness because I'm sitting right in the middle of a hell hole and it feels very dark.

I lie on my bed and let it go. Just let it go. Let it go. Stop trying to solve problems that are way beyond my capacity. Let go of the things that make me feel powerless and listen.

It's unhealthy to ignore emotions and it's unhealthy to squelch them before you have a chance to look at them. Consider them. Listen. Is your heart crying? Are you hurting? What tension are you holding in your body?

Carry Out the Heart Work

I prefer to be honest about fear, shame, pressure, and stress. I don't want to let them reign and rule over my life, but I can't ignore them either. It's unhealthy to ignore, deny, suppress or numb yourself to emotions. There is a way through that leads to peace but be careful not to force it.

For me, speaking words that describe your inner life is necessary for the process. It's part of the necessary heart work. Wounds need to be healed. Air needs to be cleared. Attention must be given to the wound so it can heal. Not self-pity. Not attention seeking. Not woe-is-me kind of complaining. But giving sufficient attention to deal with it, settle it, and heal it.

This part almost certainly includes forgiveness and surrender. Because sometimes the stress or tension is pointing to something that is out of line. Heart work is needed.

I don't have to be afraid of emotions. They signal the cries of my heart. After a hard day I return to silence. Quiet my mind. Quiet my heart. My gut usually is no longer panicking because we made it home.

My heart and mind require care, not judgment, shame or condemnation. How else will I get through this except to care for my heart and mind?

I always felt that Christianity was telling me that negative emotions are bad. They didn't tell me what to do with them. Just that I'm not supposed to have them or dwell on them.

I read an article about the Psalms once. One third of the Psalms are poems about lament.[8] The psalmists wrestle with the conflict between emotions and how we think we should feel as believers. They give us the freedom to wrestle.

Even on days like today, when danger and violence is terribly close, by the time my head hits the pillow, I'm at peace.

I repeat in my head:

We made it.

We made it.

We made it.

~Chapter Ten~
Behind the U.S. American Embassy

Life is like baseball, or is it baseball is like life?

Pearl, Amanda and I attended an English school in El Salvador called the San Salvador Christian Academy. Amanda loved the new school because she made lots of friends. But Pearl and I didn't stay in long. Pearl was the oldest kid in school and that meant no friends her age. There were only two girls that were my age. The oldest boy was younger than either of us. That's terrible news for teenage girls who like boys.

The only situation worse than being the new kid at school is being picked last for baseball, especially when you're good at it. That moment seems to last an entire lunch recess. You stand there being judged solely by physical appearance. The team captain looks you up and down, trying to determine what kind of baseball player you will be. Since you're a girl, they easily dismiss you. Though, to be honest, they've never seen you play.

∾ • ∾ • ∾ • ∾

It's a sunny day in the fall of 1977. Pearl, Amanda and I are lined up with the other students. Two team captains are picking sides. Pearl and I glance at each other. We know something they don't. If they put Pearl and me on the same team, we'll crush the other side. If they put us on different teams, then it'll be an interesting game.

We are each handed a mitt and directed to the same team. When Pearl and I glance at each other again, I see a little smirk on her face. I smile and nod.

We are playing on a small field of grass. The school building is one story and small. It sits beyond a line of tall trees: eucalyptus, I think. From the field, I see lots of dirt and parked cars.

Life is like baseball, or is it baseball is like life? We are Perezes. We put our all into it. Amanda, Pearl and I take our infield positions with knees bent, leaning forward slightly, with hands together, almost like we are praying. We don't mind getting dirty or getting hurt as long as we win. We punch our mitts with our right hands signaling that we're ready to play. Pearl throws the ball to me. It stings my hand when I catch it. She puts her whole weight into it. That's how we were taught to play.

Tosses and catches go from first to second to third base. The pitcher signals the first baseman. The other team has one adult teacher and lots of small children. It's a rather sad group in my opinion. Their team is at bat first. The first three batters come up and they are quickly put out. That was fast.

Now it's our turn. Pearl comes up to bat. Crack! The ball soars over the infield players into the outfield. A blond boy about 12 years old sits up. A look of joy crosses his face. It has just dawned on him that Pearl is on his team. He realizes his team is going to win. She runs the bases in a jog. First base. Second base. Third base. Home. Got it. Nice. The score is one to zero.

The other team's captain consoles his team. "That's okay. Just a lucky shot." But he doesn't know what we know. That wasn't a lucky shot. We can do this all day, and they're doomed.

I'm at bat next. I practice my swing with a good grip on the bat. The pitch comes. Swing and a miss. "Show them what you've got," I say softly to myself. Crack. The ball flies low over second base. I run to first base and dive on my stomach, reaching forward with my hands. Safe! The blond boy is standing up now. He's smiling and jumping up and down. I feel it too. We're going to win.

Sweat and dust. Shouts and grunts. Tosses and catches. The best part is when I run like my life depends on it. Then I crash into the catcher as he misses the ball. Score!

I lie on the ground at the end of the game. We're winners. My heart is beating so fast it feels like it's jumping out of my chest. I gasp for air. Between gasps, I laugh. I look up to the blue clear sky. My chest is going up and down and I wait a moment for my heart to calm just a little.

Pearl reaches her hand out to help me up. I'm still breathing heavy and I rest both hands on my knees, leaning forward. I can't talk. Just breathe and get your heart to slow down. Don't you love a good game of baseball? Next comes that deep satisfying feeling that you can't hold back. At school, they never put us on the same team again.

※ • ※ • ※ • ※

At home Pearl and I are regular teenagers with chores and homework. One day our parents ask us to run a simple errand. We have to walk four blocks from our house to deliver a manilla envelop and then and return home. This isn't too hard for two teenagers in blue jeans and T-shirts.

At the edge of our neighborhood, we happen to walk behind the U.S. American Embassy. It takes up the entire city block. Across the street we see the back of the embassy building. We can only see the parking lot, the black wrought iron gate and rows of shrubs. As we reach the corner, we look down the street and see three cars coming towards us. Two large black SUVs block the road with a sedan between them. They stop at the driveway to the embassy parking lot. Two men jump out with machine guns.

We stand there, our sneakers glued to the sidewalk. It is happening so fast, and yet everything seems to be moving in slow motion. As I look up and down the street, I realize Pearl and I are the only people on the street. We are alone with these men.

My heart beats wildly. I look at one man. He's wearing jeans and a tight T-shirt that highlights his muscles. He's not a soldier. He looks straight at us and keeps pointing the machine gun in our direction. The other man faces away from us. My brain is trying to process all this in front of me.

What's going on?

Will they kill us?

Oh, I realize these guys are bodyguards! They're protecting the people in the sedan. They aren't targeting us! Whew! That was a close call.

I feel Pearl lock her arm in mine and pull me forward. My attention turns away from the men on the street. We walk, step-by-step in unison.

For a second there, I see Pearl and me getting shot. In my mind, I imagine it in a flash as if it is really happening. We are going to die here on the street. I even imagine us lying in the gutter. How will our parents find us? These thoughts are ricocheting through every corner of my mind.

The next moment Pearl and I are once again walking down a street. We are running an errand for Mom.

That's how we lived for the two years we were in El Salvador. One moment we were held captive by soldiers and dodging rioters. The next moment we were clearing dirty dishes from the dining room table and filling the kitchen sink with sudsy water. This was my new life as a missionary kid. We settled into a flow of life that was fast and slow, full of adventure and boredom, survival and existence.

ஓ • ஐ • ஓ • ஐ

I like doing chores and running errands for my parents. It makes me feel important. But after the embassy incident, I feel stupid. I overreacted. But then, I tell myself the truth about life here.

Just last week the news reported that a woman named Elena Lima de Chiorato was kidnapped by men with machine guns. Right on the street where people walk, a shootout broke out. An ice cream vendor said, "It was like a madhouse. All the people started to run to protect themselves. For a minute, I thought it was an attack on the government because the shooting was so intense."[9] But the shooting was part of the kidnapping.

At the end of a baseball game, I'm out of breath and my heart is beating hard and fast. I feel my body gasping for each breath. After a close call like this, the feeling in my body is the same. My body is gasping for each breath and my heart is beating really hard. I know what to do when my body gets this way, whether from physical exertion or panic: breathe deep.

Breathe deep.

Breathe deep.

❧ • ☙ • ❧ • ☙

In time my body started to calm down. In those horrifying seconds at the embassy my mind and gut went crazy. I analyzed the situation in seconds or maybe even milliseconds. My heart was beating so fast it felt like it was jumping out of my chest. I gasped for air. Between gasps I thought fast. Run? Hide? Drop to the ground? My chest went up and down taking in deep breaths. I hate that I froze. I just stood there. Those few seconds felt like minutes. Pearl pulled me out of my frozen state. I needed a moment for my nerves to calm. I was still breathing heavily and so was she. I kept thinking if I could just breathe evenly, my heart would slow down.

❧ • ☙ • ❧ • ☙

Normally the streets felt safe. Sure, there were crazy drivers, but mostly we were safe when we were on the street. It was nice to get out of the house to run errands, buy groceries and pay bills. Maybe we would stop for ice cream on the way back. I never expected a shootout on the street in broad daylight. But life was not what I expected here as a missionary kid. I thought we would face hardships and maybe be poor. But I just didn't expect the streets in our neighborhood to be dangerous.

One of my last thoughts each night is how I ended up living in El Salvador. My parents loved to travel. They were adventurous. So even as a young girl, compared to them I felt pretty ordinary and I sure wasn't expecting God to lead us to such a war-torn place filled with shootings, kidnappings, and bombings. People there were suffering. I was too. I could barely endure. I felt shaken to my core, especially when a rifle was pointing straight at me.

୬ • ୧ • ୬ • ୧

At night on my bed I enter my evening ritual that gets me back to peace. And today I really need to find my peace. So I start by taking inventory.

Stop everything.

Sit still.

Almost like I am looking inside myself to see what's there.

Quiet my mind. Hush. Quit talking.

Quiet my heart.

Quiet.

I have to force my mind to stop. Stop. It keeps thinking.

Quiet. Quiet. Still.

I become aware of my body. I feel no pain. I'm okay.

Everything is quiet and calm in my bedroom.

I sit in the calm and enjoy the lack of crisis.

Look around the room, see how boring everything is. How calm.

Sitting in stillness.

Suddenly I feel myself let out a long and heavy sigh. Then I take a deep breath. The heaviness of the day lifts off of me. When I sit in stillness, my body releases the tension. When I realize I'm taking deep breaths, I've really entered into the stillness of the moment.

I remember that God is here with me, right in the pain. Reminding myself that God knows, and cares, and is here. This lightens my emotional load and I let out another heavy sigh.

I'm caring for my heart by giving it attention. My heart hurts and it's a fact. It won't change any time soon. Yet my heart knows it has been acknowledged.

I see you, heart.

I see you hurting.

I feel you.

Acknowledging the pain doesn't remove it, but if my heart is trying to signal that it hurts and I stop and listen, it stops trying to get my attention.

Picture this. A person standing on the side of the road beside a car with a flat tire. They are waving their arms to everyone who drives by. They are putting all this effort and energy to get someone's attention. They desperately need to get help. When someone finally stops to help them, they can stop waving their arms.

This picture of your heart waving its arms is the effort it goes through to get your attention. I know the heart doesn't have arms, but it's calling out. "I'm here! I'm stuck! I'm hurting! Things are not okay!"

When I take inventory, I look directly at my heart. It doesn't have to get my attention any longer. It can stop raising the alarm. Instead, it can focus its energy on mending itself.

The Magnificent Strength of Heart is when I check with my heart after the danger has passed. My body may be calm, but my heart still hurts. Then I delve deeper inside. What's going on? What is it? What is that feeling? That ache in my heart? I'm trying to find the right word.

Grief. In a very deep part of me, I feel a deep grieving about this world. Somehow, I know that God's heart feels the same.

I'm amazed when God speaks to me in a way that hits me where I am.

Sometimes life is a struggle and I wish I was doing better. Then I hear God speak to me in a way that bypasses my mind and goes directly to my heart. It's like an infusion of hope and strength.

God surprises me. I know these thoughts come from God because the inner peace is too obvious to ignore. I struggle and he brings peace. I fear and he floods me with his presence. I beg for deliverance and he stays with me for a while. When his presence is near, everything changes. Suddenly, I feel peace.

God surprises me. He removes the veil from my eyes and suddenly I see him. He is huge and my struggles are small. Just a glimpse of his greatness and I feel better. I don't feel overwhelmed when I have a good view of God.

Imagine a window with a view. You face a mountain, which is your suffering. Sometimes you feel like you are falling off the mountain. But you are really in a safe place. The mountain feels overwhelming and you get tired. Sometimes you just need a good view of how secure you are in relation to the mountain. When I hear from God, it's like I return to the window with a view. I see clearly my reality. God is bigger than any mountain. I need to see how secure I am with God. I need a window with a view of God in all his glory, power and immensity.

When I go to church and sing about God, I'm standing at the window. And God talks to me; I'm looking out of the window. When my mind struggles trying to figure out how to overcome the mountain, it's too much for me. I return to the window in my mind. I find strength even though the mountain is still there.

It's like your soul is thirsty and you finally get water. Or you're hungry and finally you are satisfied. It's like holding your breath and finally you exhale. It's like a weight gets lifted off you. It's like taking off a heavy backpack. Suddenly you feel relieved.

~Chapter Eleven~
Pure in Heart

All great spirituality is about what we do with our pain.
Richard Rohr, OFM[10]

Mom likes to keep up with the news. So, every day she spreads the newspaper *El Diario De Hoy* across the dining room table. It's January 14, 1978. The headline says the Nicaraguan Embassy was bombed by a terrorist group called the Peoples Revolutionary Army (ERP). We watch the news on television. The announcer describes the bombing in detail.

Evil comes as a shock to me. I'm stunned. I'm emotionally numb. I choose silence as a method of survival. To speak is to draw attention to myself. If you shout or protest you become one of the disappeared ones, *los desaparecidos*. I feel powerless, even though I know I am not.

My only escape is to think about the future. I imagine being back in the United States. I dream of a place where I can feel safe again, where I can call the police when there is danger. Not like this place where police *are* the danger. Here, government officials in uniforms scare me. They're not safe. They become my enemies when they try to kill my neighbors, and maybe even me. I find myself dreaming again. I want to get a small job when I get back to the States. I look forward to the feeling of freedom. I want to have money and go shopping. I want to feel safe when I walk down the street. I want to go to school and not have to erase the violence from my mind so that I can study. I want to be a kid and not feel the weight of war on me. War feels terrible. To this day, I still can't even find the words to describe it.

Sometimes our house is full of people and stories and laughter. And it feels like there is no war outside. For a few hours life feels normal. Other days are just draining. So much killing, loss, sadness. When you line up several of these devastating events in a row, the week becomes overwhelming. Mental strength is taxed, and I feel my feet falter. Sunday comes and we set up chairs in the dining room for worship. My heart is at an interesting crossroads. Heart, how will you respond now? After a draining week, what do you say about God?

Part of me wants to take the road of anger and blame. It's God's fault that all this is happening. "Why don't you do something, God?" Deep within me I know it is more an accusation than a question.

Another road leads to self-pity. I know I must be the only person in the world going through this awful time in life. I hate it.

A third road leads to despair. I can't take this anymore. I just want to give up. Why pray? Why persevere? Things won't change; they'll just get worse.

I close my eyes in church and contemplate the various roads before me, like I'm standing at a fork in a dirt road. One road leads to accusing God, another to accusing people that triggers my self-pity and another even accusing me. I even think about turning around and going back, which feels like giving up. The truths about God are what my heart needs to hear. In this place of killing, loss and sadness, I worship a God who is nothing like this place. I choose the road that's not easy. I turn my heart to God and open it, knowing this might be painful. Yet I'm ready to accept him and his grace. They will see me through.

God is on high and he lifts us up. God is loving and kind. He is merciful and forgiving. God is gentle and beautiful. And so, I continue with worship and sing praises to God who is my light in the darkness.

Songs like:
- No Hay Dios tan Grande Como Tu—There is no God as Big as You
- Alabare—I Will Worship
- La Cancion Alegre—The Happy Song

- Mas Allá del Sol—Beyond the Sun
- Salmos 100—Psalm 100

My heart shifts from an accusatory tone as I continue singing. There is no God as big and grand as you. I sing in Spanish, but the meaning of the songs connects to something deep inside me. And I feel so much better.

All of the worship songs center on God. The simple and comforting truth about God is that he doesn't change. These awful events don't change the nature of God. I almost feel like this place is tarnishing me. But it doesn't tarnish him. It's almost as if the worship washes over me and cleans the toxicity from my heart. After all that has happened this week, I need it. "Cleanse me, God, from all the rebels, the radicalism and the rubbish, please." When the world around me is violent and destructive, I sing about God's holiness and it feels like defiance against the enemy. The darkness tries to swallow me, but I don't give in to it. God is holy and pure. He is not evil nor malicious.

∽ • ∾ • ∽ • ∾

My journal is at the center of my relationship with God. I read the Bible every morning and evening, and record what I hear from God. At least I write what I think he says. I have few keepsakes from my childhood because we moved so often. The oldest journal in my collection is from 1978 in El Salvador.

It reads,

> Wednesday morning Matt 6:1-34 The New English Bible (TNEB)
>
> Matt 6:1,34 TNEB
>
> ¹Be careful not to make a show of your religion before men; if you do, no reward awaits you in your Father's house in heaven. ³⁴So do not be anxious about tomorrow; tomorrow will look after itself. Each day has trouble enough of its own.
>
> Night Matt 7:1-29 TNEB
>
> Matt 7:1 TNEB
>
> ¹Pass no judgment, and you will not be judged.

This sets a standard for me. I can't give evil for evil. It's not allowed for Christians to fight evil with evil. I can't use religion to get attention. Don't worry about tomorrow—each day has its own troubles, enough to fill that day to the brim. Isn't that the truth!

My relationship with God is all about peace. When I spend time in prayer and reading my Bible, I return to that place of peace.

It was during those quiet times with God that I wrestled with the internal pain that resulted from all I'd witnessed in Central America. I felt devastated. But God was in the middle of my devastation. I found him by waiting. The most magnificent strength was there all along, in the waiting. My ritual was to sit quietly in front of an open journal; it was powerful and mystical. This was my habit each evening: I looked back on the day as I tried to dust off all the trauma and the shock of it all from my memory.

※ • ※ • ※ • ※

It's January 1978. Two passages spring to life as I'm reading. I combine them together in a way and it is exactly what I need: to read with more clarity and hear directly. I turn the pages and read the scriptures. I'm not reading with my mind as much as I'm reading with my heart. I'm looking for a word from God. It's not words in the traditional sense of letters strung together to make words and words strung together to make sentences. What I'm searching for is a word that is living and applies to this moment, a word that applies to these times.

I don't hear God in an audible voice, but he gets through to my spirit. This morning I read Matthew 5. A section of this chapter is called the Beatitudes. For a second, words stand out, as if they are being illuminated before my eyes. Then suddenly they readjust to their original typeset. It's like the Holy Spirit highlights something within my spirit.

Two parts are highlighted. I write down the very words to capture the treasure. And then I think about what God is telling me. The highlighted verses are Matthew 5:8 and 5:39.

> Sunday morning Matt 5:1-48 TNEB
> Matt 5:8, 39
>
> ⁸Blessed are those whose hearts are pure.
> ³⁹But what I tell you is this: Do not set yourself against the man who wrongs you. If someone slaps you on the right cheek, turn and offer him your left. If a man wants to sue you for your shirt, let him have your coat as well.

It's interesting that of all the Beatitudes, the ones that are most vivid are:

"Blessed are those whose hearts are pure."

"Do not set yourself against the man who wrongs you."

I feel angry that I am fighting for my own survival. If I have to, I'll fight back. But how does that work when God values the pure in heart? It's interesting to read this text with the sound of bombs in the background just a few blocks away from my bedroom.

At the border, we see people some who are pure in heart and some who aren't. Some soldiers puff up their chests and intentionally make you wait. As they walk away in their olive drab uniforms, you see a glimmer of pleasure in their eyes. They feel proud that they can control the moment. They like the power that you can see in the smirks on their faces.

Other soldiers don't take pleasure in their position. You see it in their kind eyes.

One young soldier comes up to us with an entirely different demeanor. His shoulders are hunched a little and he leans forward like he is going to serve you. He smiles and apologizes for the inconvenience.

He motions with his hand. "Please take a seat, señorita."

He is humble and takes the posture of a servant. His dark eyes are kind and glisten with joy. He is pure in heart.

What kind of person am I? What kind of person do I want to be? Either the one who wants power and control over people, or the one who serves. I want to be a person who is pure in heart, but I get mad. God says, "Don't set yourself against the man who wrongs you. Be pure in heart." This is the hard part, to remain pure in heart when I am tempted to hate. But then I remember the humble soldier.

When God asks me to do something that is hard, I know the message is from him. This is not my thought. When I read, "Blessed are the pure in heart," those words stand out once again. It's hard to be pure in heart when I just want to simmer in my anger. What do I do with the injustices in El Salvador? Letting my anger and fury consume me is not an option. I must guard my heart. I think it means that when I hurt because I see suffering, I can't let my heart get hard. If I get a calloused heart, I might be tempted to do really hurtful things. Somehow, I have to find a way that when I *do* get hurt, I will not harden myself.

∽ • ∾ • ∽ • ∾

Mom and Dad decide we should use the bus to get to school. Early one morning, Dad takes Pearl, Amanda and me on the bus to show us the right bus stops.

Right as the bus passes the front of the university, Dad points to it through the window. "That's the University of El Salvador."

As we pass, I see large five-story buildings. There are a lot of them. The modern buildings fade from view.

When we come home after school, Mom is frowning. She's upset.

"There was an assassination at the university," Mom says.

"What? When?" Dad asks as a slight frown darkens his face.

"Today. Right around 7:30 in the morning." Mom bites her lip. "Isn't that the same time you were on the bus with the girls?"

"That's exactly the time we were in front of the university. How did we miss it?" Dad's eyebrows stretch high with surprise.

Mom shakes her head, "I don't know how safe it is to let the girls ride the bus to school alone."

"Everyone rides the bus," Pearl says.

Mom crosses her arms, "I know. But, Noe, do we want the girls to ride the bus?"

It's another Sunday morning. Anger rises up inside me because now I can't even ride a bus to school. The assassination was so close, and the terrorists killed all the witnesses. We can't figure out how we missed it. Mom and Dad are talking about homeschooling us. We'll never leave the house. My world feels like it's getting smaller. Right when I'm a teenager and interested in going out into the world more, I can't.

We gather for worship. Instead of letting my heart get sucked into the darkness around me, my spirit resists. I sing out in worship to God. My every song and musical note rises in defiance to sorrow and heartache.

I focus on God, heaven, truth, beauty, faith and joy. I'm shouting at death. "I don't buy it! You are not going to suck the life out of me." I sing with great emotion and depth, the tears in my eyes are my resistance. I turn my heart towards God and focus on him, not what is happening on the earth. Violence gets so much closer to home that we can't even go out. In worship I turn my attention away from how I feel in the present darkness.

I willfully exalt and adore God who is not bound by evil. Worship takes me above all this—it's transcendent. My perspective shifts when I think about God's greatness, beauty, perfection and holiness. I join angels to honor God. My spirit merges with them.

I'm surrounded by violence that dishonors God and people. Last year there were three kidnappings and two assassinations. I've seen more weapons in my short time in El Salvador than I've seen in my whole life, except on television. In this context, I choose to honor God in worship and it's subversive. This is where I feel the strongest sense of freedom, power and joy.

∗ ∗ ∗ ∗

I learned to bury my heart and distract my mind with school and books. I read *Joni, The Hiding Place* and *When You Run Out of Fantastic, Persevere.* Sometimes my heart couldn't feel anything. I was standing strong so long I couldn't feel the pain anymore. There was too much pain all around me like a tropical shower with quarter-sized droplets. God tells me to be pure in heart; that means even if I hide my heart I can't allow bitterness into it. And I go in search of my heart to reconnect. Heart, how are you? Where are you? Come out. Don't hide any longer.

My journal is where I am completely honest with myself. It's where I face the hard things in life. I look right at them and admit how hard it is. If I don't face the hard things, they become a weight I carry. If I face them, the weight lifts. It's the way I maintain peace in my life.

One day Dad returns from the immigration office. He is angry and says, "I lost my peace." He's been preparing paperwork so that the government will formally recognize our church. I see him hunched over his manual typewriter for hours. He has a little bottle of correction fluid and occasionally I hear a little cursing under his breath. After the trip to immigration, he needs to be alone. I don't know if he prays or what he does, but I have the feeling he is searching for peace.

With my journal in front of me, I stop to see the state of my heart. If I'm hurting, I admit it. If I'm struggling, I face it. If I'm grieving, I cry. It's the intimate part of the journey where life becomes real. It's the place where I feel the most pain. It's the place where I get raw. I am aware of what happens in my internal life.

I'm alone on my bed reading a story about Jesus and the words jump off the page. "His heart went out to them," it says in Matthew 14:14. It's not the story that touches me, it's the words. And they don't jump off the page in a dramatic way. I feel my spirit stir within me right as my eyes are on these words and not any others.

> Sunday morning Matt 14:1-36 TNEB
> Matt 14:14
>
> ¹⁴When he came ashore, he saw a great crowd. <u>His heart went out to them</u>. And he cured those of them who were sick.

I flip the page of my journal to the last night's reading. I had the same stirring when I read,

> Saturday Night Matt 13:1-58
> Continued from morning Matt 12:25
>
> ²⁵And Jesus knew their thoughts and said unto them: Every Kingdom divided against itself is brought to desolation and every city or house divided against itself shall not stand.

Later that evening, I felt another stirring with the words in Matthew 15:32. Jesus called his disciples and said to them, "I feel sorry for all these people."

> Sunday Night Matt 15:1-39 TNEB
> Matt 15:32a
>
> ³²ᵃJesus called his disciples and said to them, "I feel sorry for all these people..."

I think about it. I've felt three stirrings in my heart. I combine all three thoughts and it's like a message in a bottle that connects the dots.

> *Jesus' heart went out to them.*
> *He knew their thoughts.*
> *He feels sorry for people.*

I roll over on my back and stare at the ceiling. Jesus knows what I'm thinking, and he feels bad for me? He sees that we are going through all this terrible violence and his heart goes out to us? I close my eyes and think deep about this. Life is bad when you must go through something terrible, but to think that God cares, that means something. It would hurt worse if he didn't care.

Jesus cares.

Jesus cares about people in pain. He cares about me and the people in El Salvador. My heart is comforted by the idea that Jesus' heart goes out to me because he knows we are going through a painful time. I take a deep breath. Long exhale. I'm not alone.

Jesus cares about people in times of war. He cares about people who suffer. Those who are sick and in pain. I carry these words with me over the next few days. Jesus cares about me.

Jesus cares about a teenager growing up in uncertain times. Jesus cares about a foreigner in this country. Jesus cares, about a girl with brown skin. Jesus cares. Here. Now.

Magnificent strength of heart is when you are strong enough to face the pain and brave enough not to discharge your pain onto other people. It takes fortitude and tenderness. It means being real and raw with my heart. At times I'm required to be tough minded. I hold all the emotions inside. But when I am alone with my journal, it's like I exhale. All the emotions I've been holding in are released.

My journal is open in front of me and I feel bare because I can't lie to God. I can't fake it with him. He knows everything, always. It feels like God has been stripping everything away these last couple of years. Everything that makes me feel secure.

Stripping away my culture, my language, my friends, my school, my teachers, my neighborhood and my English church community. All I have left is my family and God. I used to have friends to lean on, but I don't have any here. That's the hardest part.

It isn't easy to have a pure heart, one that knows pain sees injustice and stands up strong. I am still standing with my tender heart and my bold will and Jesus. And I dare to believe that still there is good in this world.

~Chapter Twelve~

Kidnappings

*Guard your heart with all vigilance,
for from it are the sources of life.*
Proverbs 4:23

Alone in the living room, I look out the front window with my head leaning against the glass. Past the wrought iron fence is the street with big, thick drops of rain the size of quarters splashing on the pavement. The house across the street has a beautiful rock retaining wall with steps that lead up to the house. I look at it and try to memorize it. Someday I won't be here, but I want to remember what it was like to be here.

I begin to pray. "God, I'm confused. I don't understand why you brought us here. I want to go home. Please take me away from here. Please." I expect hardships and poverty by being a missionary kid, but I don't expect terrorism and kidnappings. I feel guilty because I have a passport and citizenship in another country. I have options and choices Salvadorans don't have, especially the poor. And especially Ana. How can we leave her and escape? I feel guilty. I want God to take me away from all the suffering, not just me, but everybody in El Salvador.

※ • ※ • ※ • ※

The newspaper headline reads, "Insinca." The newspapers are all abuzz about the kidnapping of Fugio Matsumoto, a businessman from Japan. Armed Forces of National Resistance (FARN) is claiming credit for the kidnapping.

The whole family is sitting at the table for dinner, including Ana. She bought pupusas, a Salvadoran dish that looks like a stack of thick corn tortillas. They are stuffed with pork or white goat's cheese and they are delicious.

All three of us girls squeal, "Pupusas!"

Dad rubs his hands together and offers a quick prayer. We pass around the plate with stacks of pupusas, followed by a plate with cabbage and salsa.

For a moment the only noises are the clinking of plates as everyone serves themselves. Nothing is better than fresh ground corn made into a thick tortilla and cooked over a fire. It's even better when it's stuffed.

Pearl says, "I love when we have pupusas. Thanks, Mom."

I ask Dad, "What is Insinca?"

Dad is thinking and then he says, "They are a clothing company that manufactures uniforms—"

Mom interrupts. "They are in the news because their president, Matsumoto, was kidnapped. He's a businessman from Japan. It's become very political because the terrorists are demanding the release of 33 political prisoners in El Salvador."

Fugio Matsumoto was the 54-year-old president of Insinca (Central American Synthetic Industries), a textile firm. The newspaper said, "On May 17, 1978, while leaving his office at day's end, he was abducted by seven armed members of FARN. In return for his safe release, the kidnappers are demanding immediate freedom for 33 political prisoners in El Salvador. Matsumoto's family tried to appease the kidnappers by running full-page FARN advertisements in the daily newspapers, but the rebels, thus encouraged, fired off more and more demands."[11]

By June 22 the group is demanding freedom for an additional 104 prisoners, while calling for a $4 million ransom payment for Matsumoto. The kidnapping news carried on for months with bold headlines regarding Insinca. But then there were the rumors that Matsumoto had already been killed.[12]

"Are terrorists kidnapping foreigners now?" I ask.

As if Pearl reads my mind, she says "I thought they only targeted rich locals."

Dad clears his throat. "They kidnapped four of our neighbors, even the lady next door."

"What? The one who has a house just like ours?" I remember her floor plan was exactly like ours but flipped.

"The nice one who gave us a tour of her house?" Amanda points to the wall we share with her and leaves her mouth open.

"They think that all foreigners have money, but they will get a big surprise if they kidnap a missionary from the States," Mom says.

After our meal, I walk quietly across the tiled living room floor past the kitchen to the patio outside. I needed a moment to get a grip. Usually I can hold my emotions inside me, but this time I feel like I will burst.

The laundry hangs on the line. I look up to the blue sky and I want to scream, but nothing comes out of my open mouth. I grab my head with both my hands. I think to myself:

I can't take this anymore!

In the silence, I let out a long exhale, straighten myself and wipe my tears. Then I walk back inside with a lump in my throat.

༄ • ༄ • ༄ • ༄

On November 24, 1978, five members of El Salvador's radical FARN kidnap Frits Schuitema, the 34-year-old Dutch manager of the Phillips Electrical Company. The terrorists first demand a $1 million ransom for Schuitema. Then they raise the stakes on November 26 after a rival group—the Proletarian Guerrilla Army—falsely claims credit for the kidnapping. In its second communication with authorities, FARN demands $4 million from Phillips Electric, plus international publication of the group's political manifesto in major newspapers.

Negotiations apparently continue and FARN spokesmen announce they received $1 million from Phillips Electric on December 26. They confirmed that their communique had been published abroad. However, despite these concessions, the guerrillas now declare Schuitema will not be released until newspapers in El Salvador picked up the manifesto. A compromise was reached four days later, and Schuitema was released on the night of December 30, after the FARN message was broadcast via Dutch Overseas Radio.[13]

∽ • ∾ • ∽ • ∾

I hate lying. Pearl and I walk into the dining room where Mom is standing. Mom points to the newspaper on the dining room table. She looks over at Amanda who had her back to us. She flips the papers over and puts her finger over her lips. I know what she means. Don't let Amanda see the newspaper. Now I'm curious.

Pearl and I are being homeschooled now. Mom is talking about our school schedule.

"Yeah, Mom, we heard you. We must be at our desks at 8:00 in the morning."

Amanda is looking at Mom as I reach over to get a peek at the paper. Pearl looks over my shoulder. The headline is about the kidnapping of a nine-year-old Japanese girl. Now I understand. I look into Pearl's eyes and there is a connection. We don't nod but give each other a knowing glance.

Mom talks with a tone in her voice, like we are in trouble. "Just because you study at home doesn't mean you can sleep in. I don't care if you are sitting there in your pajamas, as long as you are at your desks at 8:00 sharp." She is distracting Amanda.

Mom doesn't want Amanda to hear about the story of the Japanese girl. Her father is a businessman. The story is too close to home because Amanda is also nine years old. So, I never talk about it, but that night I cry in my bed.

I don't want Amanda to hear me. She lies in the bed across from mine. I hold my cries inside without making a sound, just warm tears coming down my face. I hold the tension in my throat until it starts burning. It's the only way I can figure out how to keep quiet and cry hard at the same time.

Sometimes I sniffle. If Amanda hears me, I'll tell her it's my allergies. But she's not paying attention. I think she's already asleep.

So, I imagine a little girl who has been kidnapped. Then I think about it more. What would I do if I were kidnapped? What am I willing to do? How far would I go? Would I kill someone so that I could live?

I lie thinking in my bed. Suddenly I stop crying. If Pearl and I are kidnapped together, it's a whole different story. Pearl and I fight well together. With teamwork, we can take down a grown man—maybe more. I grab their feet, while she tackles them. This is what happens when your dad loves football, your sister loves to wrestle and you are a Perez.

If I am kidnapped alone, it would be much harder. I imagine being locked in a dingy room. I don't mind crawling in the ducts of a house. I've already done that. I don't mind sneaking up on the roof. I've already done that. I don't mind hiding in cabinets. I've done that, too. I haven't gone without food and water, though. Thirst and starvation would be tough. However, I have walked for miles under the hot sun in Guatemala. (That was before we received the van as a gift.) But how does anyone prepare for something like being kidnapped? Or looking a captor in the eye and wondering if I will be his next victim?

The hardest part is thinking about killing someone. I wouldn't mind hurting someone. Pearl and I get into fights and we hurt each other. It happens when you're active. We bruise and scratch each other when we wrestle.

Dad taught me that if you put three pounds of pressure on a knee, you can break it. I imagine being on the floor and using my legs to break the knee of an evil kidnapper.

It's the inner wrestling that is the hardest. I have endured a lot of suffering in sickness because of my asthma, and there's that unsettled feeling with violence. But the inner turmoil of cognitive dissonance is the most disturbing. I struggle with myself.

I see what is happening around me, and I don't want any part of it. I believe myself to be someone who will not crush people with coercion and manipulation. I refuse to resort to violence. I want to be part of the solution and not the problem. I swear! (And I never swear.)

I get so angry at the government and the terrorists who make the streets unsafe with their fighting and bickering.

I agonize. Do I kill to survive? It doesn't seem right. But sometimes I want to fight. If I'm kidnapped, would I kill to escape? I don't know; it's an awful thought. This is a terrible and hard decision to make. If I am kidnapped, I would try to escape and kill people if I had to. My first thought is to disable my captors and even break their knees. Three pounds of pressure against a knee—just like Dad said. But, if that doesn't work, I'll kill them.

Is deciding to kill someone the same as actually killing them? Jesus said if you hate a person it is the same as murder. But I don't hate terrorists, I just want to protect myself from them.

No, wait, be honest. I hate it. Well, no, I don't hate them. I hate it, the darkness that infiltrates my very being because I am in the throes of violence, of uprisings, of terrorism.

I hate the feeling of oppression, like my spirit is being choked. I hate the fear that hangs over this city like a cold heartless fog. I hate not feeling safe in this city. I hate not feeling safe in my own home. I hate the feeling that I don't have choices. I hate feeling trapped.

At breakfast the next morning, I pour milk on my cereal and Mom says, "What's wrong with your neck?"

"What?" I pretend like I don't know anything. "There's nothing wrong with my neck."

Mom says, "You look swollen. There might be something wrong with your thyroid."

I don't want to tell her. I've been crying all night to the point that my throat burns.

"You need to get your thyroid checked. Your Adam's apple is sticking out. I think there is something wrong. Remember that the next time we take you to the doctor," Mom says.

I look down at my cereal. I hope no one sees how vulnerable I feel right now. I swallow hard and say as confidently as I can, "Okay, okay. I'll get my thyroid checked."

❧ • ❧ • ❧ • ❧

Inner peace is the absence of turmoil and agony, plus holy presence and perspective. I know what happened last night. How I cried. How my body reacted. And I felt the burning in my throat. I calm myself with a full-on conversation in my head. I switch back and forth between reasoning with my mind and listening to my heart. How do I distinguish logic and emotion among reason, heart and spirit? Is there a way to be sure? I don't know.

I feel terror and agony. For a while my heart is heavy with this overwhelming turmoil. Then my fears begin to subside with this rush of comfort. I know the turmoil is passing. I no longer feel condemned to have such feelings of anxiety nor do I feel ashamed about having them. Through what is commonly called a "peace that passes all understanding," I'm no longer calling my faith into question.

My body has had all kinds of terrible reactions: heart racing, sweating, shaking, nightmares and that burning in my throat. Give my body time to recover. It's the same when I run. After I run, I rest. I take deep breaths and let my heartbeat slowly return to normal. Then I find peace in my body where I recover to a tranquil state—all is well

My gut was the part of me that was the hardest to handle; it screamed at me. It told me to hide, yell, run! Do something. It was agony to endure my gut's reaction and force my mind to ignore its commands. To force my body to be still, quiet. Force my heart not to believe my gut. The agony of just sitting there with my gut screaming at me and my body reacting was torture.

Finding peace at the end of the day begins when I reach that place where there is no turmoil, no agony in my mind, heart, body and spirit.

I can't calm my mind down if I continue to replay thoughts like: I'm going to die or that my family will die. The one thought I struggle with the most is about being kidnapped. Dying doesn't bother me so much. You get shot and bleed to death. You're gone.

Kidnapping. That's different because it's the captivity that's so terrifying. It's confinement, imprisonment. I can imagine feeling tormented because I have so many questions. How will I eat? How will I find a bathroom? Where will I sleep? Will they lock me in chains or tie me up? Will they beat me? Will they rape me? Repeatedly? How will I escape? Do I hurt them back? Fight? Do I stop them from killing me and kill them? If I escape how will I find my way home?

It's hard to have a mind at peace when I'm trying to decide if I should kill someone or not. Inner peace after the burdens of the day are lifted. I'm in that place where my gut stops screaming. My mind stops racing. My heart has calmed my emotions. My spirit feels the presence of God.

Through God's help, I find inner peace without burden of oppression nor fear from today. When I listen to my spirit, it's like listening to a whisper. I get an impression about something. I hear a prompting in my mind, "You will write your story." I think about that thought that feels almost foreign. I didn't have the thought. I heard it in my head and it definitely wasn't audible. And it wasn't me.

I don't feel like this is my story. It's our story. It happened to us. By that I mean it happened to my family and to the people in San Salvador: the lady next door and all our other neighbors, friends, and the church community. It happened to all of us, not just me.

The story about my inner life struggle. That's mine. The stuff that goes on inside is my story. The questioning. The wrestling with God. The internal struggle. That is my story.

I end with a prayer of gratitude. Thank you, God, that no one got shot today. No one got kidnapped. Thank you that my family is still with me. And thank you that I can breathe. In Jesus' name, Amen.

~Chapter Thirteen~
Close Call

I wanted to be stronger than the pressures of life. I wanted to be a better person. To do this, I had to take ownership of my inner life cause it's where our life flows out of.
Danielle Bernock[14]

On days that life is quiet and normal, it is wonderful for a moment. Then we hear the news and feel devastated yet again. The bombs come one after another, to the office of Mayor of Nejada, to the National Conciliation Party headquarters in San Vicente, and to the Mayor of San Miguel. People's Liberation Forces (FPL) claimed responsibility for the bombs, and they assassinated policeman Jose Saul Lopez Viera in Jiobasco. Rebels target the government. This violence is not in San Salvador, the capital. But it still gets to me when I read the newspaper headlines about yet another bomb.

Every time there is another bomb or assassination, I feel the sting of reality. I am not the master of my domain. Good is not in control. Evil is in control. I'm uncomfortable and at a loss. I feel powerless and I hate feeling this way. I long for normal quiet days.

It's dark outside and I'm lying in bed trying to sleep. Usually I fall asleep easily, but tonight I feel, what is the word? I can't even find the word in English. Inquieta, oh yeah, that's it and it means disturbed. I toss and turn in bed.

I need a good book to take me away. I love stories of people who are brave, who face tremendous odds and come out stronger on the other side. I'm reading a book called *Joni: An Unforgettable Story* by Joni Eareckson. I'm 15 years old, she's 18. I love that she is open about her inner world. She doesn't hide that she's mad at God and even wants to kill herself at one point.

◈ • ◈ • ◈ • ◈

During dinner I'm excited to say, "I'm reading a book called *Joni*. It's about a teenager who broke her neck in a swimming accident. She grew up to be an artist and draws by putting the pencil in her mouth."

"That is amazing," Pearl says. "It's hard enough trying to control your pencil with your hand. It must be really hard with your lips."

"She asked God, 'Why has this happened to me?'"

Mom responds, "Don't ask why, ask why not. If troubles are happening to people all around you, why not you? This is happening to everyone, why not Christians?"

As if to lighten the mood, Pearl turns the conversation. "Dad, what are you reading?"

"I just started a new book by Watchman Nee, a Chinese teacher."

"Mom, what about you?" Pearl turns the conversation to Mom.

"Agatha Christie, of course, my favorite..."

The conversation moves on, but I'm still thinking about what Mom said. As always, she makes me think. People always ask God, "Why is there suffering?" And, of course, Mom has to ask, "Why not?"

✧ • ✧ • ✧ • ✧

At night, I lie on my back and feel the restlessness in my stomach. I fix my pillow and settle in on my side. But I can't get comfortable. I take a deep breath. Usually I just give my body time to calm down and it does. But now my stomach feels jittery.

I can't sleep. I let out a big sigh. It's hard enough to get through the days. I don't want to struggle to get through the nights. I don't know what is happening to me, but I don't like it.

I have an idea. If I have trouble sleeping, I'm going to lie here and praise and thank God. Even if it takes me two hours to fall asleep.

I start thinking of Joni and how she follows God even though she's a quadriplegic. I begin by not counting the proverbial sheep, but by counting my blessings.

"Thank you, God, that my arms and legs work. Thank you that I'm not sick. Thank you that I'm alive today. Thank you for breath and life. Thank you for Mom and Dad. Thank you for Pearl, Amanda and Ana. Thank you for the food we eat every day. Thank you for the Bible where I learn about you. Thank you for school and how I get to go to school when some kids don't."

I start yawning. I don't know how long I've prayed; I don't think it has been hours. I fall asleep. I love my new plan. A few days of praying at night and my insomnia fades away.

☙ • ❧ • ☙ • ❧

My parents are off to yet another meeting. Pearl and I are sitting at our desks on the landing. Both of us sit facing a star chart posted of the wall. The chart marks our school progress. With my head tilted down, I'm trying to figure out math. I hear the doorbell, but I'm completely engrossed in my studies.

Ana's light footsteps come up the stairs. In a low tone, Ana says, "Go hide. There are soldiers at the door." When we are doing schoolwork, Ana is in charge of the house, including things like answering the door.

Amanda is home from school. The three of us scatter in different directions. I run to my bedroom and open the door to the wooden built-in closet. As I enter the shelves on the left. I climb behind the piles of folded clothes and move them to create a small wall to shield me from view. My body is curled up tight.

I strain to hear voices or footsteps but all I hear is my heart beating in my ears. My heartbeat feels so loud and I'm afraid others can hear it. My heart is racing and the rush in my body is so intense. I wait. I take deep breaths. I keep strict control over my thoughts. And still my heart will not calm down. I don't know how many minutes goes by, but I stay frozen and endure. Every inch of my body is telling me to run, but I can't. My mind takes over and tells my body to be still.

I hear Dad's instructions in my head, "Don't give away your position. Don't be stupid."

I'm breathing heavy and it feels so loud. I'm sure I'm going to mess this up.

Don't move. Be quiet.

I rest my head on my arms and think. Now, I don't feel safe in my own home.

It is quiet and dark in the closet. Time passes slowly.

Finally, my heartbeat returns to normal, and my body starts to ache because I haven't moved for who knows how long.

It feels like two hours have gone by, but it could have been just minutes. Ana calls out to us. I walk down the stairs as quietly as I can in my bare feet. Amanda had been hiding in the downstairs bedroom. I don't know where Pearl hid. I breathe a sigh of relief.

Ana talks with some neighbors later. She learns that our house was surrounded by soldiers. They were protecting the wife of the President. She was visiting the elementary school behind our house.

܄ • ܄ • ܄ • ܄

Facing life and death situations takes strength, to endure the moment as well as the aftermath of emotions.

Earlier today, I felt shaken. I thought I was going to die. I sit in the emotion of it. It's painful. Just raw stinging pain. I'm not a child waiting for someone to rescue me. I'm facing adversity with all my strength.

I close my eyes. Endure. Take it. It's life. It's my life. And then, with a big sigh, I release all the heaviness of the day. I say to myself, "That was a close call. It's over now." Then I open my eyes and look around my room. It's quiet. Boring. And I tell myself, "The danger has passed. I'm safe." I didn't know the term *mindfulness* at the time, but I developed some practices that included being mindful at the end of a stressful day.

Was I overreacting? Was I being stupid? When Ana first told us that the soldiers were guarding the president's wife, immediately I felt stupid. I overreacted. But then, they were soldiers, and we didn't know why they were surrounding our house.

I reflect on what happened today while sitting on my bed in front of an open journal. I still feel stupid about my reactions. I need to think. Earlier in the day all these thoughts were going through my mind so fast. Now it's evening and I try to break it down. In my internal dialogue several voices begin to emerge. Logic tells me it's reasonable to think that when soldiers surround our house, we might get killed.

When Amanda was a toddler, maybe two or three years old, she loved to dress herself in different outfits throughout the day. When we returned home from errands or shopping, she would peel off layers of clothes and leave a trail behind her: shoes, socks, tops, and bottoms. She disappeared into her room and emerged wearing a new outfit.

It was the same for me at night in El Salvador. I would go into my bedroom and peel off all the layers of fear, tension, chaos and violence from the day. And I'd put on a different robe. I'd take off all the violence that the world had thrown at me that day. And I would put on peace. Sit down, pray, read my Bible and encounter God. I would tell myself, "You are okay now. You are safe now. That was a close call."

My room was quiet and boring and luscious with peace. It felt so good to have a moment in regular everyday life without having to hide from rifles, guns, or military personnel.

I would open my Bible and my journal. Then pray, "God, what is it that you would tell me today?" Sometimes I could feel God nudging, telling me something. Other times I wouldn't. The response didn't matter as much as the practice of quieting myself down and letting go of all the tension of the day and sitting with Jesus, who is called the Prince of Peace. Sitting next to him and feel peace come over me.

Years later I was talking to Christian counselors about my experiences. I told them all of my traumatic stories. I had two counselors. They both said I should be more messed up because of what I experienced as a child. I really attribute resilience to this practice of taking a spiritual inventory of the many blessings I did have despite my surroundings. My ritual was returning to a place of peace every night.

It didn't remove the Post Traumatic Stress Disorder (PTSD) unfortunately. The PTSD affected me physically and had to be resolved. But this practice did something to give me strength for the moment.

The violence of that day, I faced it and was strengthened. I didn't carry violence from yesterday to today. Like the scripture says, "So then, do not worry about tomorrow, for tomorrow will worry about itself. Today has enough trouble of its own."[15] It took a bit of practicing that teaching. Some days were very violent. Other days were boring.

Some days that had violence upon violence upon violence and then the next day would come. I couldn't carry yesterday's violence with me into the next day because it was too much—too much for the following day.

I guess some people call that mindfulness, others would call it centering yourself. I didn't know those terms, but it was my practice. In my mind, I was doing the Christian practice of daily devotions, praying, reading the scriptures and journaling. But in developing those daily routines was this other exercise of being in the moment—being in a quiet moment to gather myself. Soaking in the quiet and the calm after a close call.

~ Chapter Fourteen ~
# Factory Bomb

If we live, we live for the Lord; if we die, we die for the Lord. Therefore, whether we live or die, we are the Lord's.

Romans 14:8

I don't want to die, that's for sure, but this verse in Romans 14:8 gives me hope. In El Salvador, sometimes I pace back and forth downstairs when I'm alone. I walk from the living room to the dining room and back. I say to myself, "I'm not going to live to be 18 years old." I feel anxiety in my gut and alarm about my present circumstances. Too many close calls. I don't know if I'm going to make it.

Christian teachings tell me how to die. If I live, I live for the Lord. If I die, I die for the Lord. Since I am in a situation where I don't know if I will live or die, these words are good for my soul. In a way I feel like I can't lose because my living or dying is for the Lord. I belong to him in my living and my dying. There is a certain freedom in these words. They can kill me, but they can't destroy me, the real me.

In other words, I want to survive, *but I don't have to.*

The spirit that is inside me will return to God. The terrorists can harm me for a moment, but that would be all, just a moment. In fact, if they kill me, they will send me straight to God. And that will be like going home.

I understand heaven is a place with no tears, no fear and no destruction. It is a place of perfection, splendor, harmony and love. Part of me wants to go there now. I would love being in a place where there are no more war.

My situation is not so scary when I think about death in this way. It really helps that Mom talks about death so casually. She doesn't understand why our culture isn't willing to talk about death and dying. "Death is part of life," she says. We have all talked about our funerals and our last wishes. It's okay. So, I have come to a deeper understanding of survival. It isn't just about that moment. It is also about what comes after.

⊰ • ⊱ • ⊰ • ⊱

Mom is direct when she talks about death. She says, "I don't know why people say things like 'they passed on' or 'they are no longer with us.' I'm not going to tiptoe around it. Why can't they come out and just say they died?"

"If your dad and I get killed," she says, "call the Lopez family. They will send you out of the country." Pearl and I know where Mom and Dad keep the passports and important papers. We know to pack lightly.

Mom and Dad plan for the worst. It gives me a feeling of security to know what to do, just in case. When we go out of the house, Mom and Dad don't walk side-by-side anymore. They explain their distancing strategy: "If one of us gets killed, at least you'll have one parent left."

Mom is matter-of-fact when she talks about her funeral. She insists, "You better not wear black at my funeral. I want my three girls to wear red!" She says it with a smile, but she's serious.

"I want my life celebrated. And you better not cry." She points her finger at us. "Don't give me flowers when I'm dead. I can't enjoy them if I'm dead. I want them when I can enjoy them."

We talk about life and death. We each describe what we want for our funerals. I want to be buried in jeans.

∞ • ∾ • ∞ • ∾

It's 1979. Mom says I can move into the downstairs bedroom. Pearl and I have been fighting a lot recently. I don't even know why but we need a break. My new room is modest with a dresser and a bed. I keep candles in my top drawer in case of a blackout. I've decorated the back of the door with magazine pictures of surfers and skateboarders. Mom doesn't like it.

"Why do you have pictures of naked men?" She asks. Mom is so funny.

I respond, "They aren't naked, they're surfing."

Mom smiles and swipes her hand in a motion that says, "Oh, never mind."

One day Amanda and I are watching TV together. Suddenly the window starts to rattle. At almost the same time the TV and lights turn off. The house shakes. I look at the rattling window and wonder if this is an earthquake. Then I hear a huge explosion which continues to shake the whole house. Is this a bomb? Maybe the courthouse around the corner is being bombed.

My first clear thought is to get both Amanda and me to safety. Mom will know what to do. My mind rushes with a stream of questions. Did we get bombed? Is anyone hurt? How bad is it? How close is it? Did it kill anyone? Is my family okay?

I can't see Amanda, but I speak to her in the dark. "Come on. Let's go find Mom. I have candles in my top drawer."

Like a blind person, I reach my hands forward and feel my way around my drawer. I find a candle and the matches. Amanda stands next to me as I light the candle. Then she takes my arm and we make our way up the stairs in the dim candlelight. My heart is beating fast. It's dark and I'm afraid.

As we enter their room, I ask, "Did you feel that?"

"Yeah," Mom says. "Are you okay?" She looks to Amanda and then to me. Mom, Dad and Pearl are present.

"We're fine," I say, as Amanda walks over to Mom.

"Are you okay, Mom? Dad? Pearl?" They nod.

Everyone says "Yes," and I can see that knowing look in their eyes. Here we are again, in a moment of devastation. Terrorism is touching our home.

We gather in the middle of Mom and Dad's room. It seems to be intact. We are holding on to each other in a small circle.

Dad cautiously looks out the window.

"Stay back," he says as he breaks off the circle.

Mom follows him to their balcony, which faces the front of the house. Coming back inside, Dad says, "That was a bomb. It looks like it's some blocks away."

For a moment, I check reality. Everybody in my family is okay. They missed us this time. Suddenly I feel a massive sense of relief because we survived.

With the electricity out, it's pitch black. There is an eerie silence. I wander out to the balcony. Above the two-story houses I see a fire darting above the rooftops in the distance. My relief fades and I feel a great sadness. Huge flames jump up to the sky in bright contrast to the darkness.

In the silence, a woman screams. She sounds terrifyingly close. Her screams come up from the depths of her soul with an excruciating sound. I have never heard a sound like it before or since. I stand there in my bare feet in horror and speechless. A flood of raw feelings overwhelm me. I feel a paralyzing horror on behalf of the screaming woman. I hear her inexplicable pain. I swallow hard. Everything is silent except her screams. I don't know her, but my heart hurts to hear her cries of anguish. I feel myself shaking.

It is torturous and shocking to hear the screams of someone in agony, then realize you can't do anything about it. I understand selfishness, and I can handle it. Insidious and wicked oppression is beyond my comprehension and it insults something deep inside me.

I can't believe the bomb is so far away in the distance. It shook the whole house and felt like it was right next door. Time stands still.

Mom calls, "Come inside. Let's sit down."

Hanging on to one another, we sit in a circle on the floor. Candles are lighting the room.

Mom's voice isn't shaky. "Let's play Uno. Come on. Who wants to deal?"

Suddenly cards are shuffled and I'm holding mine. We are quiet and go through the motions of the game. The usual laughter and poking at each other is missing. The fun is missing. Everything is missing. I see Mom trying to distract us and I pretend like it's working. After a few hands, Mom sends us off to bed.

ଓ • ଏ • ଓ • ଏ

Every morning I wake up to the smell of coffee. Even though I hate the taste, I love the smell and today it's especially comforting. How do you function after a night like last night? I stand in front of my dresser deciding what clothes to wear. Who cares what I wear today? It doesn't matter. It feels like my heart is numb. I go through the motions at breakfast. We all do. No lively chatter. Just quietly passing the cereal and milk to one another and the sound of clinking spoons against cereal bowls.

Mom breaks the silence. "The newspaper says it was 100 sticks of dynamite. It hit a family who lived upstairs over their business. It was a small factory with chemicals and that's why the fire was so big."

"Want to go see the building?" Dad says.

"Yeah, let's all go," Mom answers. "Go get ready."

Suddenly there is life at the table. Amanda gathers the bowls into a pile and takes them to the kitchen. Pearl grabs a wet cloth from the kitchen and wipes the table. I put away the cream and sugar. I'm thinking out loud, "I wonder what happened. How close? How many people died?"

We pile into the van and Dad drives through our neighborhood. Ahead of us is a long line of cars with people who are curious like us. It's a residential neighborhood where people park their cars parallel to the sidewalk. Along both sides of the street, I count seven cars that were burned up by the explosion. All the windows in the houses across the street are blown out. We slowly drive past the bombed-out house. The second story is completely gone. There are big holes in the walls, and everything is black. Debris is everywhere. As we pass the house, I look out the van window. I'm trying to capture images of the scene in my head as if I am taking a picture with my mind.

Dad counts, "It was ten blocks away from us."

Mom repeats the newspaper report. "One hundred sticks of dynamite and only 10 blocks from our house."

We pull up in front of our house and pile out of the van. It's strange. Our two-story house looks just the same as when we left. But the world *feels* different. A bomb explodes in our neighborhood. Only 10 blocks away. So far, they have *kidnapped* four neighbors, including the lady next door. This is the *second bomb* near our house.

I race up the steps and wait for Dad to open the steel security front door. I don't feel safe here. As we enter the house Mom says, "Go do your schoolwork. Come on, now. Everyone, get to work."

Life continues with an additional weight on me. There is reading to do and tests to take. And my heart feels heavy. I sit at my desk and pull out my goals for the week. I set my heart aside and begin again.

◈ • ◈ • ◈ • ◈

I lie in bed at night with my journal in front of me. I feel the same way I did the day of the earthquake on February 4, 1976. Shock. And I can't wake up my heart. It's stunned. I don't know how to feel. I roll over and lie on my back. I can't even think. I'm so tired.

In the morning, I wake up to the smell of coffee. My journal is still next to me. I fell asleep with my clothes on. I jump up and get ready for the day.

This morning is no different, and yet everything is different. I have a swarm of feelings whirling around my heart. It's not like last night when I felt numb. Now I feel like I'm about to burst.

I'm familiar with the feelings: shock, terror, eminent danger, outrage at the inhumane treatment of people. This urgent feeling to take control, call for justice. Lightning thoughts passing through my head:

I must protect myself. Protect others.

Be on high alert.

Think fast.

How to respond.

How to not get hurt.

How to not get killed.

How to protect the ones I love.

All are racing around in my head. I hate that sickening feeling in my stomach. Life can't be this bad—this is horrible. This isn't happening, but it is. And the nagging question is this, "Who would do this to another person?"

The clinking of spoons in coffee cups brings me back to the present. Mom pours milk into her cup until the coffee turns a caramel color, "I want each of you to pack your bags, in case we need to suddenly flee the country. And don't forget the black satchel. If something happens to your dad or me, you must remember to take it. It has all our important papers. Birth certificates, marriage certificate, passports and stuff."

"Yes, ma'am," Pearl answers. It's Pearl's responsibility to get the black satchel because she is the oldest and it's my responsibility to remind her.

"We won't forget," I say.

"Before you start school today, go pack your bags," Mom says. "And remember to keep candles in your room in case the electricity goes out again. Make sure to have matches, too."

My small bag is packed on the floor right next to my dresser. It feels like I'm in a movie. Who suddenly flees the country? That only happens to spies and government officials. We are just a family.

Dear God,

Sometimes I wish I was a superhero with superpowers. I want to save the world! I wish I could swoop down and change everything in an instant: no more war, no more destruction, no more fear, no more abuse, no more poverty and no more despair!

I don't understand why you let people be so destructive with each other. How can you just watch in silence? Doesn't this stir some emotion in you? I feel outraged. Don't you?

I feel like screaming but I don't. I hold it in, and I feel like I will explode! I wish someone could hear the cry of my heart. I don't think I can take much more of this violence. There is no safety. That is how I feel. I look for safety and I can't find it anywhere. There is no safe place. I don't think I will live to be 18 years old. I can't see it. I expect that I will die here with all the other people who are dying around me.

People are suffering all around me and no one can change it. The people who can change it are too busy fighting for power. They can't see beyond their own self-interest. Who will fight for the children? Who will save them? I feel like no one sees the suffering of children; not just my suffering but of those around me. No one cares.

I swallow my tears and keep the pain inside me. I am surprised how many people don't look you in the eyes; if they did they would see the tears. I distract people with my smile even though I have tears. They look at my mouth and don't see the pain in my eyes.

I can still hear the woman from the factory bomb screaming. I can't get it out of my mind. Everything is silent except for her screams. They echo in a chasm of darkness as big as the Grand Canyon. I feel powerless to help her. Once again, I feel such mixed emotions. My family survived; hers did not. I think the paper said seven people died, but she survived. My house is intact; hers was destroyed. I feel relieved and burdened at the same time; such is the result of hearing another person's suffering. It moves me. I shed tears for a person I have never met.

It's hard to shush my mind. It talks all the time. About everything. It's this running commentary in my head. And it has a critical opinion about everything. I just need to shush it sometimes.

Taking inventory is best done when the mind is shushed.

How's my body? I'm okay. No injuries, no pain. I can breathe deep and not cough.

How's my heart? My heart is hurting. I feel my face crinkle and my throat tighten. My heart hurts with this heavy load.

Emotionally, it's so difficult to watch warring factions: government versus terrorists and people caught in the cross fire. I don't know the people who died, but it hurts my heart that they are dying

Needlessly.

Prematurely.

Violently.

I feel the lump in my throat, and I pray, "I'm hurting. This moment is painful. Right here. Right now. And my heart is weary of the pain that doesn't go away."

I love my family, yet I fear losing them. I think about the future and wonder if we will all return home together. Will this war take someone from my family? Death creeps through our neighborhood and selects people to take.

A neighbor's house is raided. Young men are taken, and the family never hears from them again. I feel the tension especially when we are at border crossings or checkpoints. They point rifles at us. I hold my breath.

✥ • ✥ • ✥ • ✥

On Sunday we set up chairs for worship. My heart is not numb anymore; it's hurting. My heart is at an interesting crossroads. Heart, how will you respond now? After a draining week, what do you say? Do you harden?

I'm at a fork in the road yet again. One road leads to a hard heart. The other road leads to a tender heart. I can't take the road that lets my heart get hard. A hard heart doesn't care about anyone else. Let the world go to hell, just find a way to survive. Who cares? I think about how lovely it would feel to let my heart get hard. I imagine the relief I would feel. It's a way to step outside the pain.

But I have a tender heart which means I feel the pain exquisitely, my own pain as well as the pain of others. It's the price you pay for love. If you love, you will feel pain. There is no other way. I can't imagine living without love. So, the logical conclusion is that I will remain with a soft, tender heart that feels the pain. My heart is strong.

The truth is, I care. I can't let my heart get hard. God told me to be pure in heart. I can't lie to my heart. It's not allowed. I can't make the hurt go away either. As long as children are suffering, families are being bombed, and women are screaming in pain in the streets, my heart will hurt.

God wants me to be pure in heart. I worship today in church with tears in my eyes. I open my heart to God. My mouth says the truth about reality even while my heart hurts. God is true. He is good while men and women are bad. He is right and holy. I worship him because of who he is. He is the creator. Powerful and mighty.

~Chapter Fifteen~
Detained in the Country

*What is birthed in the insecure hearts of evil men
is first birthed in darkness.*
Belinda McDanel

We are traveling back to El Salvador from Guatemala. We had picked up our school supplies from the CAG. Pearl and I are studying at home, but Amanda is still attending the Christian Academy of San Salvador. Pearl and I need our supplies for the school year. The boxes in the back of the van include our books and our Paces. A Pace is a learning packet. We have to complete 12 Paces in each subject. Each one is about the size of a magazine. It includes a practice test and the actual test that Mom gives us.

The border crossing is uneventful as we enter El Salvador on the two-lane highway. We drive through the mountains. As we come and around a bend, soldiers appear. One moment we are talking and laughing. The next thing, a soldier is waving to my dad to pull over in the middle of nowhere. It's just a wide spot on a country road. The soldier in an olive drab uniform uses motions to show us where to park. We're in the countryside and no one is around except soldiers.

As Dad puts on the brakes and pulls over on the dirt road, a memory flashes through my mind. On one of our days off, we were off driving to Lake Illopango. We came upon a van in the middle of the road that was abandoned and shot up. Dad slowed down and drove around the van. We later learned that some nuns had been raped and killed.

As we step out of our van, I see the shot-up van in my mind. A wave of fear runs through me. There are about 15 or 20 soldiers. Some point rifles at us.

The soldiers are being rough with my dad. They push him against the van, like a police officer might push a suspect against a wall. Dad holds his hands up and they search him. Other soldiers start searching our van.

We stand in a line on the opposite side of the van: Mom, Pearl, me and Amanda. Mom is usually sassy. She talks back to policemen and she jokes with soldiers at the border. But right now, Mom is quiet. We all remain silent, but it is unsettling to see her being silent. I'd rather have Mom yelling and screaming and pushing us to get a job done than standing there quietly while soldiers hold us at gunpoint.

I make a mental announcement to my mind, "We are in danger." I'm hyperaware of every move the soldiers make. I remember Dad's instructions and immediately look down to avoid eye contact with the soldiers. I pray silently for God's protection. My imagination has already gone wild. It wasn't just the soldiers that scared me. It was Mom's silence. Everything moves in slow motion. I can't tell how long this takes but it feels like forever. Here I stand on a warm sunny day, birds are chirping as I look down at my sandals.

It takes all my discipline to remain still in quiet agony while my heart is beating like crazy. I want to run and hide but we're surrounded. I stand there with my head down and show respect to the soldiers who could literally do anything to us.

The soldiers talk to Dad. They continue searching the van, probably for weapons. They look at our passports and then let us go. We jump into the van and speed away.

It's strange. It seems like a small thing to be detained in the country. But it's a huge incident for me because it was menacing.

While we're standing there facing the men in their uniforms, with their rifles, holding power over us, we can't help but wonder, "Are we going to live?"

᷾ • ᷾ • ᷾ • ᷾

Each close call makes my heartbeat pound so loud I can hear it and I feel my blood pulsing in my ears. Sometimes my body shakes. In that moment I can't reassure myself with thoughts like, *"It's going to be okay."* Because I don't know.

My mind goes crazy with ideas of how this could all end. I could be shot or killed. Someone in my family could get injured or killed. This could happen in a moment.

One moment.

Moments move in slow motion. I wait in the uncertain moments with doubt, where I stand at the edge of life looking into the chasm of death. Waiting to see if it will swallow me up.

Once again, I shift into that inner chamber of my soul where I focus on self-preservation. Stay in that moment. Wait right on the edge.

I hate waiting.

I want us all to live. And I can't do anything about it but wait to see what happens next. These waves of uncertainty come and go. It's a wonder that we walk away.

When the moment passes, we check with one another. "Are you okay?" We look at each other, like we are checking to see if everyone's body parts are still there. "Yeah, you look whole."

Whew.

Waves of relief wash over me.

My heart is still beating wildly. I take deep breaths trying to calm myself down. My mind tells my heart, "The danger has passed. It's over. We made survived. It's okay. We're okay."

I take deep breaths and look out the window at the lush greenery over the mountains. The winding road has a rhythm as we sway in and out of the curves. My heart begins to calm down.

What was I thinking about before we got detained in the country? Hm. I can't remember.

It doesn't matter.

Chores, laundry, errands. Who cares? Homework that goes on and on forever. As soon as I finish one homework packet, there is another one to take its place. As soon as I take a test, there is another, then another.

When life hits you with a crisis, you stand still.

Frozen.

Life becomes different. Small things don't matter as much.

You stand there wondering at the age of 15, "Is this the end of my life?" I can't help but get the feeling that I'm not done yet. I haven't done what I am supposed to do on earth. It can't be over yet.

Suddenly I have a perspective that's divine. I have clarity. Life slows down enough to see things you usually miss. What is most important in life? Little arguments with my family suddenly seem petty. Fights over personal space are so small. It doesn't really matter who sits next to the window in the van or someone touching my things. I feel silly that we even had a whole conversation about these things. Who cares? Nobody cares. What matters is that we're alive. I have my family with me, all of them. What matters is finishing the divine purpose of our lives. God has given each of us something to do on earth. We must complete the divine purpose.

Like Paul said to the church at Rome, "If I live or if I die, I do it unto the Lord."

৬ • ৵ • ৬ • ৵

At night alone in my room with my journal, I plop on the bed. With a big sigh I release all the heaviness of the day. I'm saying to myself, "That was a close call. It's over now."

The best way I can describe my evening ritual is how I transition from darkness into light. Darkness comes around me, but I can't let it latch on to me. I can't welcome it or take it home with me. It's like a cleansing ritual from darkness to light.

I become present in my room. The room is quiet and unimpressive with pale green paint on the walls and a hint of a leaf pattern painted in forest green. Imagine crickets chirping in the background. Mom and Dad are in their room and I can hear them laughing. I'm on my bed lying on my back looking at the ceiling. It's boring. Right now, my heart and head need this quiet, boring space.

Breathe.

Breathe.

Breathe.

When we enter danger, I announce to myself, "We are in a crisis." When the danger has passed, I announce to myself, "We are not in a crisis. We're safe." I have to repeat this to myself many times to tell myself. "No one is pointing a gun at us right now." Be present. Look around the room and around the house. It's quiet and safe.

I sit with an open journal in front of me. I'm listening to wisdom from an ancient text, the Bible. God, what do you have to say to me?

I turn my attention inside. My spirit is always at peace.

I always need cleansing. Like stepping though mud and collecting the grime of the world, cleansing is forgiving those who hurt me and those who threaten to hurt me. Let go of bitterness and the desire for revenge. Let go of any toxic emotions that invite me to respond with darkness of my own. Dump negative emotions on the pages of my journal or to a close friend. Cleanse myself in worship as it gives me a fresh perspective. God is good. Life is more than my hardship. I will get through this. At the end of my life, this moment won't be as big a deal as I feel it is right now. I'm taking the long view.

My Process
- Announcement
- Get myself to think.
- Listen to my Heart—mixed emotions.
- Listen to my Head—logic
- Listen to my Gut—panic. It's over
- Spirit—peace

We could have died, but we didn't.

I was afraid. But my heart is calm now. My life could have been tragically changed, but it wasn't.

I need to pick up where I left off. I have things to do. Responsibilities, homework, chores and laundry.

My heart hurts and I feel like crying, so I cry. Cleanse my heart of all the pain. Pour out all my emotions on God. I see myself with Jesus. Like toddlers who are angry at their parents. I beat his chest and kick him, but he holds me. I pinch his face, then he soothes me with his words. He smiles in my direction.

Return to God who is good and kind; and not at all like the violent and demanding people here. When I turn my attention to God and open myself to Heavenly Father, I find peace in his presence.

~Chapter Sixteen~
Magnificent Strength

Look at your own heart. Unless I'm crazy, right now there is a still, small voice piping up, telling you as it has ten thousand times before, the calling that is yours and yours alone. You know it. No one has to tell you.

Steven Pressfield[16]

It's April 1979. The mood in our house begins to change. At the breakfast table Mom says, "When we became missionaries, we committed to serve four years in the mission field. But we need to cut this missionary term short because of the danger. I want you to start praying about going home. It hasn't been four years, but I'm asking God to provide a way for you girls to fly home."

Dad said, "When we were at the Christmas program at Amanda's school, we found a note on the van."

"What did it say, Daddy?" Amanda asks for all of us.

"They are threatening to kidnap you girls." Dad clears his throat, "We need to fly you home."

"What on earth?" Pearl asks.

"We don't have any money," I say.

"But terrorists don't know that. We're from the United States. They assume…" Mom says. "Start praying about flying home."

Wow! That's news. I have been praying for a long time to go back to the United States. I admire my parents for following their dream to travel. I never wanted to ruin that for them. But I really want to go home. Yahoo! I'm going to start praying about that!

At night, I lie on my bed with my journal open and write: Pray for flying to the States. I think to myself; can this whole ordeal be coming to an end?

In only three weeks, there is a sudden flurry of activity. On Monday, Mom and Dad contact some friends in the United States. On Tuesday, those friends agree to have Pearl, Amanda and me live with them. On Wednesday, we pick up our tickets. On Thursday, we pack our bags and say goodbye to friends. On Friday, we board a plane to Los Angeles, California.

Before we board the plane, we take pictures, pausing on our walk from the van to the airport terminal. I'm so happy to leave El Salvador, but I'll miss Mom and Dad. My sisters and I are leaving.

Mom and Dad will be staying for a while. They must liquidate most of our stuff and wrap up our lives. They plan to pack the van and drive back to the States through Mexico. We don't know when, or if, we will see them again.

We are minors flying alone. Pearl is 17 years old, I'm 15, Amanda is 10. Everything I own is in my suitcase. I had to leave my skateboard. We all had to leave some of our favorite possessions.

On the day we left, the Catholic Cathedral was bombed. Nineteen worshippers were killed. Policeman Rafael Melendez Solis was assassinated. There was one kidnapping attempt at the Costa Rican Embassy and another at the French Embassy.

We're on our way home! From the window on the plane, I see the capital, San Salvador. The streets, cars and buildings grow smaller. Soon the rooftops look like little squares of Chiclets gum. Mom's words are on my mind. "You are Perez women. All Perez women are strong. You can't help it, that's how we are. It's in our blood. As a family we'll get through this and soon enough we'll be back together again."

❦ • ❧ • ❦ • ❧

The country of El Salvador changed me. I learned about the quiet nature of the spirit. The war in El Salvador was loud. People demonstrating. Radios blaring. Newspapers blaming. Politicians screaming. Everything was loud. But spirit is nothing like that. People are loud and powerless. Spirit is strong and quiet.

Living in El Salvador was, to say the least, a transformative experience. My story is about being shaken to my core and reaching for resources I never thought my teenage soul had. I'll never be the same and I'm not sorry for that. My life is divided between before El Salvador and after.

At first, I doubted the idea of hearing from God or trusting my spirit. But I learned to hear God and to pay attention to my spirit. It's hard to describe how spirit works. It speaks like a gentle breeze, like a feather or a soft whisper. I barely notice it. The Holy Spirit speaks and is not forceful at all. The Holy Spirit is gentle and I need gentleness. It's so refreshing considering the forceful dangers around me.

Spirit is …

- Like a twinkle.
- Like a flash.
- Like an impression.
- Like a glimpse.

Then again, the Spirit quickens and it's as fast as a twinkle or a flash. There in one second and gone the next. What was that? I really have to pay attention to capture that mystical moment.

I wonder how many times I missed that glimpse into eternity. I vaguely remember other times that the Spirit spoke, but I didn't write it down. Sadly, I don't remember the specifics of those moments now. My guess is that the Spirit sent these messages a thousand times. That is what it's like. Spirit pursues me. I'm busy with my own thoughts. Life distracts me. However, I notice two things. When I am sick and when I am suffering, all the busyness of life slows down. All the thoughts in my head grow quiet. That is when I hear Spirit more clearly. And when I hear Spirit, I can hear God.

A word is highlighted as I read the Bible. Which word? The flash comes and then it's gone. Write it down quickly before I forget. Write it as accurately as possible. This is a clue and the beginning of exploring all that it means. It's a message in a bottle. Clues to help me find hope and peace in dangerous times.

Like a gentle breeze.

Like a feather.

Like a whisper.

Like the sunlight on your skin.

Spirit is gentle like a feather. Or soft like a whisper. I barely notice it. I'm hanging on to every word like it will save my life, and maybe it will.

I met God in El Salvador and he was different than I expected. He was gentle. After listening to a thousand sermons about God, I imagined him to be demanding, impatient, strict (even mean), a no-nonsense kind of God. But instead I discovered God cares about my heart. Somehow, I was able to hold what I had been told about God in one hand and what I experienced for myself in the other. I found God in whispers.

One day I stood in the dining room in El Salvador looking at some recently developed pictures and I heard a whisper. I had had them developed with square corners. This was the cheapest option. The new, more expensive option was to get them with rounded corners. I liked one picture in particular. (It appears on the back cover.) I'm on the left. Amanda is in front. Mom is holding a baby next to Pearl. In the background you can see our red VW van. I picked up a pair of scissors so I could trim the corners myself. I wanted them rounded. I heard a whisper, "Don't." By now I had come to welcome the whispers and even respond. In my mind I said, "This is my picture. Who cares if I cut the corners?" Again, I heard the whisper, "Don't." I couldn't imagine regretting such a simple action as cutting the corners on a picture. Nor could I fathom why it even mattered. So I decided to cut the corners anyway.

Now, 40 years later and I'm searching through piles for pictures to include in the book. I want a picture of the van, and I find one with nearly the whole family present. I think Dad is taking the picture. And I remember cutting the corners of the picture. This is the best picture that I have of the van. It would have been better uncut. I smile. God is gentle. He guides, but if I don't listen, he doesn't scream or punish. He lets me learn. I should have listened to the whisper. I didn't but I learned that, once again, it was right. Spirit is always right.

Even though living in El Salvador was a grand adventure, our home life was quiet. We would laugh and have fun. But at night everyone was in their own room. I would lie on my bed and try to figure things out. But oftentimes the political and social unrest was like a puzzle too big for me, a problem too difficult for me to solve. However, when I took a life coaching class at Western Seminary, they gave me the concepts to describe what happened.

According to research, our bodies have a neural network in our brain. Everyone knows that. It's your mind. But there is also a neural network around your heart and another neural network in your gut.[17] What this taught me is that there is more than one brain in your body, and they talk to each other.

Somehow, I stumbled upon this discovery when I was in El Salvador. I learned how to distinguish between the different brains in my inner dialogue. On the one hand I would express the rational, logical perspective of the mind. Then, on the other hand, I would express the perspective of my gut. "We're all going to die. We're all going to die." Finally, all my mixed feelings would come spilling out from my heart.

What is intriguing is that, when I would go through my evening ritual at the end of the day, I was listening to all the perspectives in my head, heart, and gut. At the very end of the whole process, I would hear a small, still, quiet voice. It took me a long time to figure out that it was my spirit speaking. I would listen to my head, my heart and my gut, but my spirit was always at peace. If I could manage at the end of the day to let my head have its say, let my heart have its say, let my gut have its say, then all these parts of me would calm. Then I would listen to my spirit and it wasn't afraid to die.

This internal spirit level, if I could land back at that spirit place, was always at peace. Even if I had a gun pointed at my head earlier that day, I would return to peace. I would get myself back to that place of peace and stay there. I'd look around my room. It was boring and quiet. My body was calm, my mind was calm, my heart was calm.

A strong heart is one that resides in pain, endures it, looks at it and names it. A strong heart stays in the uncomfortable moment. It finds a way to connect to God in the pain. It practices defiant worship. It worships God as good, even when circumstances are not. That takes a strong heart.

Magnificent Strength of Heart is when you add to that a strength of spirit. Strength of heart combined with strength of spirit becomes magnificent. I believe that every person has a resilient human spirit. Every person can access their spirit with practice. Every human spirit that is connected with the Spirit of God has an unlimited source of strength.

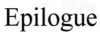

Epilogue

Our family reunited in Corpus Christi, Texas in the summer of 1979. The week my parents left El Salvador, the government officially recognized their church organization. The church still endures to this day.

Several Salvadoran terrorist groups united in 1982 to form a political party. As a group, they signed a truce with the government. The civil war officially ended in 1983.

In the fall of 1979, my family settled down in California. Pearl, Amanda and I entered public school. Mom and Dad continued serving in ministry. They entered prison ministry in 1985, where they worked until retirement in 2013. They recruited mentors for prisoners. My mom launched a program called Comadres, which matched foster parents with babies of prisoners. To encourage bonding between mother and child, the foster parents created photo albums and brought the babies to visit their moms in prison.

As adults, both Pearl and Amanda entered the medical field. I followed my parents into the ministry. All three of us married and had children. We were able to be there for each other during life's highs and lows. We all live in California within driving distance of each other.

In El Salvador, I never had time to finish crying because the incidents came so close together. It's what I call devastation in rapid succession. When I returned to the United States, I jumped into high school, then college. I was so relieved it was over. I must have smiled nonstop for a whole year. Or it felt like I did. But I had recurring nightmares that lasted 10 years. To be clear, I didn't have nightmares every night during those 10 years. I noticed that if I ever felt stressed in life, like when I was writing a paper for seminary, I would have nightmares about soldiers chasing me. I came to realize the soldiers in my dreams were a sign of stress.

In midlife, I suffered ministry burnout. I started seeing a couple of counselors. All the parts of me that had been numb came to life. I cried for two years. That is, every time I had a moment alone, I cried. They were unfinished tears from yesteryear. The grieving had to be done to lighten the weight of my heart. A kind of cleansing took place. In therapy I met supportive Christians who specialize in counseling pastors and missionaries in Fresno, California.

2009, Link Care, Fresno, California

"Remember when you were kidnapped?" the young therapist asked. We were in her little office facing each other. I was in the middle of a midlife crisis and she was just getting started in the helping profession.

I knew she was going somewhere with this question, but I interrupted her train of thought, I needed to clarify, "I wasn't kidnapped."

The therapist looked surprised. If her eyes could talk, they'd say, "Really?"

I repeated myself with emphasis and challenged her with a point of my finger. "I was NOT kidnapped. I was held against my will. There's a big difference between being kidnapped and being held against your will." I was playing with nuances of words and trying to sound funny, but my words were sobering.

I proceeded, "In El Salvador there were seven terrorist groups when we lived there. It was the *terrorists* that were behind the kidnappings. *They* took hostages and demanded payment of millions of dollars. That's how they funded their rebellion. Terrorists never held us hostage. We were held against our will by *soldiers*, not terrorists."

The therapist nodded. "So you were not kidnapped, but you were held at gunpoint by soldiers."

"Yes."

The therapist leaned forward with kindness in her voice. "Listen to yourself. Listen to your words."

My words slowly came out of my mouth. "I was held against my will."

She looked at me with a question in her eyes. "Do you hear it?"

And I repeated, "I was held against my will, but I tell myself I wasn't kidnapped. I was held at gunpoint by a group of soldiers." I swallowed hard and tears filled my eyes.

"Hold that feeling. Stay there in that moment."

My shoulders started shaking as warm tears ran down my face.

"Okay, you're ready. Let's start the EMDR." (EMDR stands for Eye Movement Desensitization Reprocessing. It's a therapeutic tool.)

◈ • ◈ • ◈ • ◈

In Fresno, I found a time and a place where I felt safe to release the emotional burden. I started telling stories to caring Christian therapists. I was still emotionally numb and clinically depressed when I started sharing my stories. My stories made the therapists cry. At first, I felt bad about that, as if I was hurting them. I hadn't thought about El Salvador for many years. I hadn't cried in a long time. The therapists taught me how to cry again. They cried for me, at first. Then they cried with me when I found my own tears. I wrote a poem about this healing in my book,

Intimate Journey: Battle Scars. The counseling sessions were a tremendous time of personal growth and healing.

During recovery, soldiers with guns returned to my nightmares. I spent about four years in counseling. All the emotion inside me, I channeled through tears and poetry. We resolved the Post Traumatic Stress Disorder (PTSD) with EMDR. After seven EMDR sessions, I stopped having those nightmares.

Being detained in the country (chapter 15) was, by far, the worst moment in my life. I wasn't just facing the possibility of death. With my family surrounded by a group of soldiers, I was aware they could hurt us, rape us, beat us, torture us. The pain. I could hardly stand the thought.

I look back to that day and wonder about God.

Where were you?

During therapy, those words came from a deep part inside me. I had never asked Jesus before, but here I was 40 years later asking, "Where were you?"

And I heard Jesus reply to me:

I was there.

I never realized that Jesus was there and saw everything we endured. His words sunk into the very core of my heart. Jesus continued to comfort me about that terrifying experience.

Spiritual power to stop evil in real life is available. But it's not all up to me. I can't intervene in a life that has never surrendered to me. I won't intervene if people don't ask.

"Are you talking about prayer?" I asked.

Yes, prayer.

That day I saw a family of five. All of them had surrendered their lives to me. All had prayed in the past. All were praying in the moment. They knew me and knew my heart.

Spiritually, sometimes things come together to make evil stop. When evil men are active on this earth, there is darkness behind them. The darkness can be stopped in prayer. Not by begging God, but by addressing the darkness and making it go. Not everyone addresses the darkness. Some pray to God and ignore the spiritual dark forces.

I responded to Jesus, "The reason this story is so hard to share is because I thought God might sacrifice us."

As if Jesus pulled back a curtain from before my eyes, he continued.

God is not like that. He sacrificed one—me. That is, he sacrificed himself; that's what love does. Love sacrifices for the benefit of another. Evil does the opposite.

Evil sacrifices another for their own personal benefit. Evil is the opposite of sacrificial love.

What I realized was that somewhere in my heart, I thought I was supposed to be the sacrifice. But Jesus was making it clear. *He* was the sacrifice. The gift.

Yes.

I'm sorry I doubted your heart.

I love all my children, both the ones with a surrendered heart and without.

A surrendered heart gives me permission to intervene. Not everyone gives me permission to be active in their life.

This is a conversation I've been waiting to have with you. I want you to know my heart.

I am for you.

I am with you.

I'm not against you.

I have no desire to sacrifice you.

Instead I want you to know and experience my love for you.

I

sacrificed

for

you.

To show you my great love for you.

I

love

you.

Then and now.

I look back and see your love for me. I didn't always feel worthy of it.

That was a lie from the enemy who afflicts people. He is the afflicter who comes to torment people any way he can.

Never in a million years would I expect that kidnappings would have anything to do with me, because kidnappings only happen to the rich and the powerful and the important people. I feel ordinary but I was wrong.

Beyond the Pages

Magnificent Strength of Heart
The Journey

Would you like to strengthen your heart?
Join Belinda's email list to learn about
the online course. Send an email with the
subject line: MSOH The Journey

bmcdanel@outlook.com

My Commitment: I will never give or sell anyone's email address to a third party. I will only use your email to notify you about articles, courses and other resources designed just for the reader.
You are free to unsubscribe at any time.

End Notes

¹ National Consortium for the Study of Terrorism and Responses to Terrorism (START). (2016). Global Terrorism Database [Data file Search 1977–1979 El Salvador]. Retrieved from https://www.start.umd.edu/gtd/
² Duley, Giles. "When a reporter becomes the story." Ted Talk. https://www.nytimes.com/1977/09/07/archives/wife-of-us-executive-is-seized-in-el-salvador.html
³ Article by Bill Howard, *Memoirs of a student: Maria Menjivar*. http://www.scopefoundation.com/history-of-the-s-c-o-p-e-foundation/memoirs-of-a-student-maria-menjivar/
⁴ Ernest Hemingway. (n.d.). AZQuotes.com. Retrieved November 30, 2020, from AZQuotes.com Web site: https://www.azquotes.com/quote/406806
⁵ https://youtu.be/T6JxQe41elU
⁶ Bernock, Danielle. *Because You Matter: How to take ownership of your life so you can really live.* Shelby Township, MI. 2019. Kindle ebook, location 1257.
⁷ Lock, S. *Share of U.S. citizens owning a valid passport 1989-2017.* March 1, 2018. https://www.statista.com/statistics/804430/us-citizens-owning-a-passport/
⁸ Ramsey, K. J. *Scriptures and Neuroscience Agree: its helps to Lament in Community*, Christianity Today, November 15, 2019.
⁹ New York Times, "Wife of U.S. Executive is Seized in El Salvador." September 7, 1977. https://www.nytimes.com/1977/09/07/archives/wife-of-us-executive-is-seized-in-el-salvador.html
¹⁰ Rohr, Richard. *Adam's Return*. New York. Crossroad Publishing. 2004. Print.
¹¹ Newton, Michael. *Encyclopedia of Kidnappings.* New York: Facts On File, Inc. 2002. Print. Page 187.
¹² Ibid.
¹³ Ibid. Page 267.
¹⁴ Bernock, Danielle. *Because You Matter: How to take ownership of your life so you can really live.* Shelby Township, MI. 4Media. Kindle ebook, location 1600.
¹⁵ Biblical Studies Press. NET Bible 2.1 (noteless) (Kindle Locations 41262-41263). Biblical Studies Press.
¹⁶ Pressfield, Steven. *The War of Art: Break Through the Blocks and Win Your Inner Creative Battles*. Black Irish Entertainment LLC. 2002. Page 23.
¹⁷ Soosalu, Grant and Oka, Marvin. *mBraining: Using your multiple brains to do cool stuff.* MBIT International Pty Ltd. 2012. Kindle Ebook. Page 26.